MANY LIVES, MANY LOVES

D0451874

By the same author

INSIGHTS FOR THE AGE OF AQUARIUS

ITALIAN FOR STUDENTS OF SINGING

MANY MANSIONS

THE MARK TWAIN PROPOSITION

THE WORLD WITHIN

MANY LIVES, MANY LOVES

Gina Cerminara

DeVorss & Company, Publisher
1046 Princeton Drive, Marina del Rey, California 90294-0550

Copyright © 1963 by Gina Cerminara
All rights reserved.
Published simultaneously in the Dominion of
Canada by George J. McLeod Limited, Toronto.
Manufactured in the United States of America
by H. Wolff, New York
Library of Congress Catalog Card Number 63–13710

Grateful acknowledgment is made to:

The Alfred Korzybski Estate for permission to
reproduce an adaptation of the Structural
Differential, from Science and Sanity: An Introduction to Non-Aristotelian Systems and
General Semantics (*International Non-Aristo-*
telian Library Publishing Company, 1st edi-
tion 1933, 4th edition 1958; distributed by
Institute of General Semantics, Lakeville, Conn.)

Alfred A. Knopf, Inc., for permission to
quote from The Prophet, *by Kahlil Gibran.*

Fourth paperback printing, 1987

ISBN: 0 – 87516 – 429 – 3

Printed in the United States of America

*"Love is a thing to be learned,
through centuries of patient effort."*

D. H. LAWRENCE

Contents

MANY LIVES, MANY LOVES

1

A MATTER OF LIFE AND DEATH
Reincarnation and Hell

A liberal Protestant minister whom I know has given a good deal of consideration to the idea of reincarnation and finally he has come to accept it. One day I asked him if he ever makes so bold as to mention the subject to his parishioners from the pulpit. "Well," he said, "only very seldom, and very cautiously. The last time I did I referred to the theory of reincarnation, compared it to the theory of hell, and let them draw their own conclusions."

I have often thought of this remark and reflected that it represents a substantial step forward in the thinking of mankind. Though a minister who dared make such a statement would still meet with indignation and even dismissal in the majority of Christian churches, there was a time not so long ago when he could not have said such a thing in *any* Christian church. Disgrace and even imprisonment or death would have been his fate in an earlier age had he dared to speak of so heretical a notion as reincarnation, and, worse yet, placed it dispassionately on the same level of intellectual consideration as a dogma of the church. That was the time when anything known on the authority of the Church and Bible was not to be called in question.

But times have changed drastically. Though thousands of people still continue to regard traditional theological certainties with unthinking veneration, thousands of others have been shaken in their beliefs by the magnitude and scope of Space Age discoveries, and by new disclosures of anthropology, semantics, and comparative religion. They have come to realize that the scientific method cannot be properly used in one department of thought and totally disregarded in another. They have become aware of the fact that the Bible has passed through the hands of many copyists, translators, and policy-minded churchmen, and may be remote from the original intent of its transcribers. And it has become increasingly apparent to them that Christian theology was conceived in an age more intellectually circumscribed than our own and may be far removed from the true spiritual import of what Jesus said and did.

Some of these people have discarded all religion in disgust because they believe it is decadent and see only exploitation in the uses to which it has been put. But others have felt that in the midst of the chaff there may still be some wheat. And they have been willing to approach religious beliefs with the interested and open-minded curiosity that characterizes the scientific spirit everywhere. The minister who proposed to his congregation that both hell and reincarnation be regarded as theories, and weighed for their respective merits, is a worthy representative of this attitude.

It is no trifling matter to think of theories of human destiny at this particular juncture of history. It is, in fact, if I may say so, a matter of life and death. . . . Far more than we realize, our treatment of our fellow creatures, our daily conduct of life, our private and our public decisions, and therefore our destiny and the very destiny of the planet on which we live, depend very intimately on the manner in which we view the ultimate questions of life and death.

There may be nothing, after death.

Or there may be heaven or hell.

Or there may be reincarnation.

The Nothingness theory is widely accepted, not only by Marxists in Communist countries, but by most psychologists, psychoanalysts, and intellectuals in our own country. But I would prefer to limit my discussion, for the moment, to what the minister suggested, and draw a comparison simply between the theory of hell, as commonly thought of by Christians, and the theory of reincarnation.

Considered as a theory, the concept of hell as an everlasting place of fire and punishment has many outstanding difficulties. Most of these difficulties have been seen, and protested against, by thinking people for centuries. How can a God who is, as we suppose, a God of Love send a soul to everlasting torment? Could any mother be so unfeeling? And could God be less compassionate than a mother? And how can a soul which is, as we define it, a nonmaterial thing be in any way affected by fire and brimstone?

But even if we overlook these basic and really major discrepancies, and assume for the moment that maybe hell and heaven really do exist, there then arise many other problems of considerable magnitude. Approaching the matter in the spirit of serious ethical and psychological inquiry, we are confronted first of all with the fundamental problem of selection, or, to use a more theological term, of judgment. After death, who is to go where, and why?

In the East there is a fable about a monkey who was very devoted to his master. One day the master was lying asleep under a tree and the flies that alighted on his face caused him to twitch in his sleep. *I must kill those flies!* thought the monkey. *They are disturbing my master's rest.* So he picked up a large dry branch from the ground nearby, and with all his might bore down on his master's forehead, killing all the flies, and killing his master too. . . .

How sincere the monkey was! How considerate! How kind! And how stupid. . . .

All too frequently well-intentioned people are similarly lacking in common sense. A good motive is surely more creditable than a bad one; but unless it is acted on intelligently, it can lead to disastrous results.

Now if we assume, as all good Christians must, that St. Peter is in his traditional place as doorkeeper at the Gates of Heaven, we cannot escape the question: How will he properly judge human souls who, like the monkey, commit well-meaning but tragic blunders? Should they be judged by their good intentions? Or by the mischief they unwittingly cause?

If you say an act must be judged by its intent, then all of heaven must be filled to overflowing with millions of well-intentioned fools, who will inevitably become painful if not ruinous company to all the well-intentioned souls who happen to be intelligent. And if you say an act should be judged by its consequences, then many a pure-souled, pure-hearted blunderer will be doomed to everlasting fire and brimstone down in hell—a fate which certainly seems unfair.

This, then, is one basic ethical difficulty in the heaven-hell theory—a difficulty which only pious and unrealistic vagueness can overlook.

But psychologically there are difficulties still more formidable. Assuming that kindness of heart is a trait necessary for admission to heaven (and it would be difficult to imagine a heaven where people were unkind) precisely how much kindness will be considered necessary? We all know people who are kind to their mothers but unkind to strangers, or kind to strangers only provided their skin is of the same pigmentation as their own, or kind to people in general but unkind to cats, or kind to anybody, but only when it is not inconvenient.

Surely the Heavenly Board of Entrance Examiners must be even more percipient than we are of the gradations, nuances, and muddy admixtures of kindliness with baser elements in the human heart; and surely, so that St. Peter can make just and uniform decisions, they must have settled upon some basic standards concerning admission. Possibly they have done as personnel psychologists do, and devised a rating scale for every virtue, with degrees from 0 to 10. At what degree of kindness then could a person be considered eligible for admission? Points 1, 2, 3, and 4 might well be deemed too low; but if they set the eligibility minimum at Point 5 (medium kindness of heart) would not the Point 5 man feel somewhat less than adequate in the company of Point 6, 7, 8, 9, and 10 men, or, more especially women? And might not this lead to feelings of frustration and inferiority which surely have no place in paradise?

Truly, whenever we begin to give any psychologically realistic thought to the matter, it soon becomes apparent that St. Peter's job, as popularly conceived, must be impossibly difficult. Even assuming that heaven may (by now) be equipped with microfilmed records, an IBM card system, precision scales, and electronic computers, decisions as to who does and who does not merit a place up there could, by any sensible criterion, only result in one injustice after the other. Heaven and hell provide only two eternal alternatives for a being whose nature is so complex and graduated as to require something equally complex and graduated to accommodate it. Even the Purgatory of the Catholics, providing as it does a third possibility, does not meet the requirements adequately. Any competent writer of drama or fiction takes into account the complexities and subtleties of human nature. It is only in Class B movies and television scripts that all the characters are either Good Guys or Bad Guys. Surely it would seem unbecoming to attribute to the Author of the Universe an arrangement which has verisimilitude only for the minds of children.

There is not only the question of the complexity and the graded nature of man's qualities; there is also the question of the dynamics of causation which make him what he is: his heredity and his human and cultural environment. Do the Eternal Judges have no psychological insight into such matters? No realization of how being born in the slums, of alcoholic and degenerate parents, is far more conducive to a life of crime than being born in a house of culture, to parents who are responsible citizens?

By all these counts, and many more, the theory of hell—and its correlative, heaven—is disappointing to any rational mind. It has had the merit of frightening people into good behavior, as heaven has had the merit of enticing him to good, and therefore can be said to have some utility at least. But unfortunately hell has frightened, and heaven enticed, all too few, and all too little. The sway of heaven and hell over human hearts can never be reestablished, despite the overwrought emotionalism of popular evangelists, precisely because the average man of our times is no longer in the frame of mind to accept inconsistent, illogical, and factually unverifiable systems of thought. The methods of science and the spectacular success of science are too widespread in the consciousness of modern man to admit of a return to the naïve faith of our fathers.

Church attendance and church membership may have numerically increased in the past decade; but this is probably due far more to a prevailing nervousness about the state of the world than to any genuine convictions about the truth of traditional Christian theology.

There exists, however, an ancient concept about the human soul and its destiny which in modern times has made a surprising reappearance not only in literary and philosophic works but also in experimental sessions dealing with the mind, namely, the concept of reincarnation. This is an idea about man and the universe which, unlike the heaven-hell theory, has some degree of evidence to substantiate it.

Reincarnation is the theory that the human soul evolves

slowly through a long succession of lifetimes. To anyone who finds the theory of evolution reasonable, there should be no great difficulty in finding reincarnation reasonable also. By this theory the basic evolutionary idea is enlarged in two important respects. First, it states that the evolution is of consciousness as well as of form. Second, it affirms that each life unit's existence does not contribute merely to the ongoing evolution of a species; it contributes also to its *own* evolvement. It signifies not only a structural advance, but a psychological and a spiritual one. It operates under laws as exact as those of physics, its most fundamental law being that of *karma,* or cause and effect, action and reaction. This means that a person is born in any lifetime in exactly the set of circumstances and with exactly the hereditary endowments appropriate to his merits and demerits of character, as established in previous lifetimes. "A man is born into the world which he has made," as the Hindu proverb puts it.

By this theory the well-meaning soul who blunders and wreaks havoc in another man's life will not be sent to everlasting torment. He will instead be sent back to planet earth where, through becoming the victim perhaps of someone else's stupid blunderings, he may gain insight into the criteria of common sense behavior, and where, by being faced once again with the practical difficulties of life, he will gradually learn better judgment.

By this view kindness of heart or any other multidimensional trait of character is not measured by a two-dimensional yardstick, or "judged" for all eternity on a pair of balances that have been unequally weighted to begin with.

It is seen rather as the particular stage of growth of a gradually unfolding consciousness; and its future state, like that of any other growing thing, is exactly dependent on the state of its growth now.

The reincarnation theory, then, unlike the heaven and hell theory, allows for the gradual unfolding of all beings with regard to all qualities and all capacities. It takes into account complexities, gradations, causation. It does not result in logical impasses, ethical contradictions, or psychological absurdities. It is in short the most reasonable of all possible theories that try to account for human life, death, and destiny. The irony of the situation is that its adherents, in our time and in our hemisphere, are regarded as members of the lunatic fringe, whereas actually the theory is far less lunatic than the dogmas of Christian orthodoxy.

So in one respect at least reincarnation could perhaps be compared to alcohol, about which someone once said that it may not be a good cure for a cold, but at least it is the cure which fails most agreeably. To those skeptics and materialists who say that there is no explanation for human life, I would say: You may be right. So be it. But if reincarnation fails, too, as a theory, at least it is the theory which fails most reasonably. . . .

Reasonability, however, is not all there is to commend the reincarnation idea. Many thousands of people have accepted it in the western hemisphere on the strength of its reasonability alone. But in the present century there has appeared considerable evidence to substantiate the logic of the idea.

Thus far the evidence has been of two major types: evidential clairvoyance and evidential age-regression hypnosis. The two best known examples of these have been the clairvoyant data of the great American psychic, Edgar Cayce, who died in 1945 after 43 years of remarkable work; and the sensational Bridey Murphy case which attracted world-wide attention in 1956.

Of the Cayce material much has been written.[1] It has brought conviction about reincarnation to some people and to others it has not. But it has given impulse to thought and study even where it has not brought total conviction, and it has inspired research which has in turn brought conviction to those who had previously been skeptical.

One of the many who read the Cayce material thoughtfully, but with doubts as to its veracity, was Morey Bernstein of Pueblo, Colorado. Bernstein was a businessman, with university training in economics and business; but by avocation he was an able hypnotist. Dubious as to the truth of reincarnation, he was none the less willing to experiment. He knew a young woman in Pueblo who was an exceptionally good hypnotic subject. In a hypnotic session to which she agreed, Bernstein suggested that she go back in time beyond her birth. She proceeded to relate a lifetime in Ireland of the past century about which she provided a number of obscure but, as it turned out, historically accurate details.

The book which Bernstein wrote on the case reached bestseller lists two weeks after its publication. It was immediately attacked by the orthodox in both religious and scien-

1 See the author's *Many Mansions* and *The World Within*.

tific quarters, and the tactics used in discrediting it were nothing short of shocking.[2] Facts were either suppressed entirely or distorted beyond recognition. Items were invented or stretched out of true proportion to make it appear that all the presumed memories could be accounted for in the present-life childhood of Ruth Simmons, the subject of the experiment. The general public, misled by the specious reasoning, the ridicule, and the falsification of the opposition, within a few months lost interest in the case, though in actuality no one ever really succeeded in explaining away the historical items which Ruth Simmons produced.

Since then many other hypnotic age-regression cases of the Bridey Murphy type have appeared, with similar substantiating evidence in historical records. But these have been reported, if at all, only in newspapers and none of them has as yet been made the subject of a serious psychological study. Some of these cases were those of laymen; others were those of professional hypnotists or psychotherapists.

Unfortunately most of these professional persons have not wished their interest in so unorthodox a subject to be publicly known. In my own personal acquaintance I can count fifteen practicing psychiatrists and psychotherapists

[2] For an analysis of these distortions and of the intrinsic value of the Bridey Murphy case in the opinion of a professor of philosophy, see: *A Critical Examination of the Belief in Life after Death*, by C. J. Ducasse (C. C. Thomas, publishers, Springfield, Ill., 1960).

Watch also for the new edition of *The Search for Bridey Murphy*, scheduled for late 1963 (Doubleday and Co.), which is to contain rebuttals to the attacks made earlier.

who privately are thoroughly persuaded of reincarnation. They even go so far as to work therapeutically with patients who also believe in it, in a reincarnationist frame of reference, and they achieve results as effective as those obtained by any other theoretical point of departure. But, lest they lose their prestige with their colleagues, they say nothing openly about their belief, their clinical cases, or their research in this area; and as a result much valuable substantiating data lies buried in private files.

There is one psychiatrist, however, who has had the courage not only to do active research in reincarnation, but to publish his findings as well. This is Dr. Ian Stevenson, head of the Department of Neurology and Psychiatry of the School of Medicine of the University of Virginia, who has for many years been collecting psychologically relevant data. It is his published study, in fact, which provides us with a new and unexpected type of evidence which may ultimately prove to be the most unassailable evidence of all: the actual *memory*—in waking consciousness and without hypnosis—of a past life, on the part of many people.

This will come as a surprise to those persons who, in objecting to the theory, raise what they consider to be an insuperable difficulty. "If it's true," they will say, triumphantly, "why don't people remember their past lives?" Such skeptics are usually not sufficiently well-read to know that both in antiquity and in modern times there have been many persons who have reported a distinct memory of a past existence; or—if they have, in fact, read about such cases—they have read them with unseeing eyes or have shrugged them off as tales so palpably absurd as not to merit serious thought.

Their skepticism is perfectly understandable. I myself do not believe in the theory of hell, and I would still not believe in it if somebody were to tell me solemnly that he had been there, that he remembered it well, and that he had conversed while there with several of my less saintly friends and relations. This last detail might add plausibility to his story but none the less I would, frankly, discount the whole silly tale and conclude that the man was either drunk, deluded, piously overimaginative, or deliberately lying.

It is understandable then to me how a cultivated person, reading by chance that Pythagoras spoke explicitly and in some detail about several of his past lives, could dismiss it as being an exaggeration or an invention characteristic of the Age of Fable. Finding that Thoreau believed he had lived in Judea at the time of Christ, he would naturally ignore it as the poetic overstatement of a man who had lived too long in the woods on a diet principally consisting of potatoes, molasses, and beans. Learning that Salvador Dali believes himself to be the reincarnation of St. John of the Cross, he would almost unavoidably dismiss it as an affectation of an artist noted for his eccentricities.

So for a man to say he recalls a past life, and even to produce a few colorful details concerning it, is of itself unconvincing. It is unconvincing even to me, and I am not by any means a materialist skeptic.

But there are past-life memories and there are past-life

memories, and sometimes, surprisingly enough, it has been possible for the claimed memory to be substantiated, at least in part.

The classic case of this type is, of course, the well-known case of Shanti Devi, a young woman still living (as of 1963) in India, whose well-authenticated past-life memories have been so often reported that I hesitate to recite the story once again.[3]

The typical features of this kind of case are as follows: A person (usually a child) says that he recalls a previous lifetime here on earth and relates a number of details concerning his former home, his family, his personal appearance, the manner of his death, and other specific items including names of persons and places not knowable to him through any published account or any other ordinary means. Then, when the matter is carefully checked, many of these details are exactly confirmed.

Obviously a person who claimed to remember a former lifetime as a well-known personage—say Johann Strauss or Frederick the Great—would not provide the best type of example inasmuch as there is too much information in print about both personalities which the person could conceivably have read, and forgotten about, or which he could have picked up clairvoyantly. The case in which a person claims to recall a lifetime in ancient Greece or Babylon of some obscure person about whom nothing has been recorded is also, clearly, unsuitable simply because there is

[3] See *The Search for Bridey Murphy* (Doubleday and Co.), p. 103, or *The Challenge of Reincarnation*, Charles Luntz (Luntz Publications, St. Louis, Mo.), pp. 46-48.

no possibility of verifying it, however true it might conceivably be.

The best type of case, then, for the purposes of evidence, is that in which the presumed memory is not about a famous or a much written about person, but about a relatively obscure person who lived recently enough for some checkable traces of his lifetime to remain.

The case of Katsugoro, first reported by Lafcadio Hearn, may be considered representative:

"A Japanese boy called Katsugoro, when about eight years of age, stated that he had been called Tozo in a preceding life a few years earlier. He claimed to have then been the son of a farmer called Kyubei and his wife Shidzu and to have lived in a village called Hodokubo. He further stated that Kyubei had died and that his mother had then married a man called Hanshire. He said that he himself, Tozo, had died of smallpox at the age of six, a year after his father had died. He gave details of his burial and described the appearance of his former parents and their house. Katsugoro was eventually taken to the village he named and the persons he named were found or identified as having lived there. In the village (unaccompanied by anyone from the village) he led the way to his former parents' house and recognized it and them. He pointed to a shop and a tree in the vicinity, saying that they had not been there before which was true. Altogether, Katsugoro's statements provided sixteen items correctly matched with the verified facts of this case." [4]

4 "The Evidence for Survival from Claimed Memories of Former Incarnations," Ian Stevenson, M.D., *The Journal of The American Society for*

This case is one of 44 similar ones that Dr. Stevenson had collected up till 1960. He presented and critically examined them in a two-part article published in a scientific journal in that year. Twenty-eight of these cases seemed to him for various reasons to be particularly strong; in these cases six or more items of information volunteered by the individual were subsequently verified.

Dr. Stevenson considered a number of alternate theories that might account for cases of this type. Racial memory, for example, might be proposed as the explanation; or extrasensory perception into the memory of a living person; or possession by a discarnate entity. Admitting that such explanations might conceivably account for some of the cases, he concluded however that the most plausible hypothesis for others was clearly reincarnation. In the conclusion of his article he stated that he did not think these cases *prove* reincarnation, but that the evidence does justify a "much more extensive and more sympathetic study of this hypothesis than it has hitherto received in the West."

Since the publication of this historic paper, Dr. Stevenson has continued his search for similar instances of memory, and, on a trip to India and Ceylon in the summer of 1961, came upon some very remarkable ones. On the basis of these he has made a number of generalizations. He has found, for example, that childhood seems to be associated with a much higher incidence of past-life memories, the majority of the spontaneous recall cases in his collection having occurred in children under ten. A strong emotional

---

Psychical Research, Volume LIV (April and July, 1960), Nos. 2 and 3. Reprints are available for 50¢ from the A.R.E. Press, Virginia Beach, Va.

experience, especially those connected with death (as by murder or execution) seems to favor recall in a subsequent life. He has also found that hypnosis, states of reverie or meditation, and certain drugs such as LSD (lysergic acid diethylamide) seem to promote recall.

In addition Dr. Stevenson has set up certain criteria for the analysis of such cases which can be helpful to other investigators. He stipulates, for example, that the child should show no evidences of mediumistic ability; that a written record of the statements of the child should be made before verification is attempted; that the verification should be made by independent persons, unrelated to the child; that the items recalled should be highly specific; and that the facts remembered should not have been written or printed in any one book, although it may be permissible for the verified facts to have been published in several books.[5]

The study of apparent past-life memories is an entirely new departure for the study of reincarnation, and one which promises to be extremely fruitful in the years to come.

Dr. Stevenson is not the only psychiatrist who has found LSD to be of great psychological significance. LSD is a chemical derivative of ergot, a fungus which grows on rye and other cereals; and like the psychedelic mushrooms to which it is related, it causes extraordinary changes in per-

[5] Since Dr. Stevenson's interest in reincarnation has become more widely known, a number of American cases have come to his attention. He is interested in receiving accounts from persons who believe they have a past-life memory of this evidential type, and he may be written to in care of the University of Virginia, Charlottesville, Va.

ception and awareness. About 10 per cent of the persons who take it have what might be called the equivalent of a mystical experience. Telepathic experiences frequently occur, and there seems to be a heightening of clairvoyance in those who already have the gift somewhat developed. Therapeutic benefits have been widely reported, including some spectacular cases of alcoholism and dope addiction which have cleared up with only one or two dosages. In the experience of a group of Canadian investigators about half the cases of chronic alcoholism studied—including many persons who had tried Alcoholics Anonymous without success—showed immense improvement as a result of the LSD experience. The behavioral change was apparently related to deep changes in values, motivation, and self-insight made possible by the psychedelic session.[6]

There is a rapidly growing technical literature on LSD, and yet much of the data is still unpublished, including many cases which seem to have reincarnationist implications. I know personally of one extraordinary case in which the subject—a friend of mine and a college instructor in English—seemed to relive, in agonizing detail, a very dramatic lifetime in ancient Egypt. As a vestal virgin who broke her temple vows of celibacy and secrecy, she saw her newborn child strangled by the priest and was then herself buried alive. The outcome of the experience was the complete and immediate clearing up of a psychological difficulty of two years' standing.

[6] "The Use of LSD-25 In the Treatment of Alcoholism and Other Psychiatric Problems," MacLean, J. R., MacDonald, D. C., Byrne, U. P., Hubbard, A. M., *The Quarterly Journal of Studies on Alcohol*, Vol. XXII (1961), pp. 34-45.

I know of other cases less dramatic, in which people merely seem to see themselves in the costume and the surroundings of other epochs, and are left with the conviction that it was an actual memory. Unless such seeming memories could be afterwards confirmed by tangible facts such as those we see in Dr. Stevenson's cases, we would of course be unable to consider them as valid memories of the past.

In other cases people have no such apparent memory experiences under LSD but come away from the experience with an inner conviction that all life is one, and that every individual life constantly renews itself. Among such cases perhaps no more striking example could be found than that of Jane Dunlap, whose book *Exploring Inner Space* should be required reading, in my opinion, for every psychologist, theologian, and theological student in the country.[7]

In her LSD sessions Mrs. Dunlap recapitulated the whole evolutionary process, from amoeba to man. She seemed to relive with intimate immediacy, often with violent physical reactions, the desperate struggle of every little life unit to survive, and she emerged with the conviction that "always after death there had been life. . . . The fact that He arose from the dead is considered important only because we have forgotten what each of us really knows deep inside: all life dies and lives again. . . ."[8]

Elsewhere, in a published magazine article, Mrs. Dunlap

---

7 (Harcourt, Brace, and World, Inc., N.Y., 1961). "Jane Dunlap" is the pseudonym of a writer famous for her books in another field.
8 *Exploring Inner Space,* p. 41.

more specifically states her realization, from LSD, that evolution is not something that occurred millions of years ago, but is going on here and now—that it is the very meaning and purpose of our existence; that every person is at a slightly different stage of evolution; and that reincarnation is a process whereby the Divine Glass Blower remelts old glass, as it were, and blows new forms of ever-increasing splendour.[9]

Whatever one cares to make of such experiences, it is clear that the tiny limits of man's conscious mind are being extended and transcended in strange new ways; and the experiences he is having will require a new systematic world view to accommodate them. As yet LSD has not provided what could be called evidence for reincarnation; but it may well be that, separately or in combination, it may soon provide yet another avenue of approach to the whole problem of substantiation.

The case for reincarnation, then, is certainly far from established in any strict sense. It has not been "proven" in a manner that would satisfy a rigorous materialist. But this much can be said for it: the theory is logical. It is plausible. It is congruent with two widely accepted scientific propositions, that of rhythmic and cyclic recurrence—observable in all phenomena of nature—and that of evolution. As a theory it accounts for more facts in man's observable mental life than does any other theory, including that of heaven and hell.

It has commanded the respect of many thinkers who would not even regard the heaven and hell theory worthy

[9] *Fate* magazine (June, 1962), pp. 29-30.

of philosophic consideration; and there are at least three types of circumstantial evidence which seem to support it. Thousands of people have reached the point of conviction on the strength of this much alone, and I have no hesitation about admitting that I am one of their number.

Those of us who take this position are, of course, not considered very respectable in academic circles. But I believe that very soon we shall be vindicated by Capital S Science, and that in the retrospect of fifty years, or less, we will finally be respectable. Perhaps we may console ourselves, therefore, with being retrospectable, at least. . . .

2

Reincarnation and Clairvoyance

The majority of people in the Western Hemisphere regard reincarnation as a preposterous superstition, and clairvoyance[1] as an impossibility. To attempt therefore to demonstrate the reality of reincarnation through the evidence of clairvoyance would almost seem the equivalent of trying to prove the existence of a pixie on the testimony of a leprechaun.

But a thoughtful person must recognize that new knowledge becomes available through new instruments of knowledge. The world of the very small was not accessible to mankind until the Dutch spectacle maker Janssen invented the microscope. The world of the starry heavens was only vaguely known to us until Galileo, Kepler, and others perfected the telescope. It stands to reason that realities beyond the reach of our senses need to be explored by methods that go beyond the reach of the senses; and regarded in this light, the attempt to explore the possibility of reincarnation through clairvoyance may not seem so idiotic an undertaking.

[1] *Clairvoyance,* from the French, seeing clearly; the direct perception of distant events or objects by means other than the senses.

To do so we would have to begin, of course, by first establishing clairvoyance as a valid instrument of knowing. This is not nearly so difficult a task in the second decade of the second half of the twentieth century as it would have been in earlier decades.

In recent years more and more universities have established parapsychology laboratories in which such matters as telepathy, clairvoyance, and other Psi faculties (as they are now called) are being systematically studied. These include not only the pioneering institution, Duke University, but also the University of New York (formerly called City College), the Universities of Oxford and Cambridge in England, the University of Alberta and King's College in Halifax, Canada, and, perhaps most noteworthy of all, for many reasons, the University of Leningrad in Russia. Several branches of the armed forces of the U. S. Government have been given substantial grants for the investigation of these matters also, the implications of supernormal faculties for the concerns of national defense and the space program having been recognized for some time.

It is significant that the primary emphasis of most of this research is no longer on "proving" the reality of telepathy and clairvoyance. Their reality has already been established to the satisfaction of researchers in the field, even if it is still a matter of suspicion and scorn to many academic psychologists. The emphasis is on discovering such things as: What environmental conditions are most favorable for the Psi experience? Can any internal or external agents (such as mushrooms, peyote, LSD, hypnosis, strobe lights, the Faraday cage, etc.) be used to heighten the faculty?

What personality types score highest in ESP tests? Can the behavior of animals (such as cats, who often find their owners' new home over long distances of strange terrain) shed any light on the ESP faculties of man? And so forth and so on.

But laboratory experiments of this type move cautiously and slowly. The actual use of clairvoyance as a systematic tool of knowledge has not yet been attempted (so far as I know) under strict controls in university psychology departments, though it seems likely that the armed forces and the space program have this possibility clearly in view.

In any case the very real usefulness of clairvoyance in matters of practical concern has already been demonstrated many times outside the confines of laboratories.

I am not referring here to those many thousands of well-attested cases of spontaneous clairvoyance (or telepathy) in which a person has a dramatic single paranormal experience, such as a mother seeing a vision of her son at the moment of drowning many thousands of miles away. These experiences come unbidden, usually in moments of stress, danger, or the death of some much loved person; and the individual has no power to command a similar experience to come again.

I am referring rather to those individuals who can use their clairvoyant faculty *at will*, and who have done so over a period of many years for the assistance of other people in the solution of their problems.

People gifted in this manner have existed throughout history. In some cultures they have been highly regarded,

as were the oracles of ancient Greece. In others they have
been persecuted as witches. In our time and place, for historical reasons which need not be gone into here, they have
been scorned by the intellectuals out of disbelief, and by
orthodox religionists out of the fear of trafficking with the
devil.

In the twentieth century we have had several outstanding examples of practicing or professional clairvoyants,
the most famous of which is undoubtedly Edgar Cayce.
Cayce's medical clairvoyance has been reported so many
times that it hardly seems necessary to reiterate it here.
The reader can refer to several biographies[2] and a number
of magazine articles about him. Any qualified investigator
can himself go to Virginia Beach, Virginia, and inspect at
first hand the documented records covering a life work of
some 43 years. Cayce's ability to see into the human body,
describe its condition, and suggest modes of cure is so well
attested both as to its accuracy and as to its dramatically
helpful results that it can hardly be disputed by any careful investigator.

One reason why the work of Cayce has made a considerable impact on many modern minds is that the people
around him had the good sense to record stenographically
everything that he said, and to keep careful files of the
"readings" with all correspondence and subsequent testi-

2 *There Is A River*, Thomas Sugrue (Henry Holt, 1953); *Edgar Cayce,
Man of Miracles*, Joseph Millard (Spearman, London, 1961); also a 33⅓
long-playing record: NBC's Monitor National Radio Show on the Edgar
Cayce Story, a collection of 15-minute interviews with people who knew
Cayce's work at first hand. Available from the A.R.E. Press, Virginia
Beach, Va.

monials. Most gifted psychics do not take the trouble to do this, and consequently, though their work may be both highly accurate and highly efficacious, it becomes as ephemeral as that of a cook.

But the performance of other contemporary clairvoyants has been well observed, and it is of special significance, I think, that members of the police profession have been some of the most attentive and interested of observers. It is of special significance because police officers are not given to looking at the world through rose-colored glasses, nor are they likely to be easily taken in. Exposed as they constantly are to fraud and chicanery, villainy and murder, policemen are more inclined to be hard-headed skeptics than credulous believers as regards human behavior. Yet in many places in the world police officers have sought the counsel of clairvoyants, and many crimes have been solved on the basis of information given them through psychic perception.

This cannot be said about all police departments, of course. In the first place psychics of this particular talent and of sufficient reliability to be consulted in such matters are relatively rare. In the second place, human factors of ignorance and narrow-mindedness are present in police departments as well as anywhere else, and outmoded laws regarding fortunetelling under which many honest psychics may still be arrested and fined undoubtedly affect and circumscribe the thinking of police officers in many places. But despite all this, a sufficient number of criminal cases have been solved for police departments through

clairvoyance or its related gift, psychometry,[3] for us to recognize that here is something not merely theoretical in
nature, but intensely useful for the practical concerns of
life.

The clairvoyant Mme. Lotte von Strahl, now of Los
Angeles, was for many years of assistance to the police of
Berlin, Bremen, Aurich, and Oldenburg.[4] Frederick Marion helped solve a number of crimes in various capitals of
Europe.[5] Gerard Croiset—who has been studied by professors at the Parapsychology Institute of the University of
Utrecht and has been the subject of several scientific
reports—has solved many crimes for police departments in
his native Holland.[6] And another Dutchman, Pieter Van
Der Hurk—better known as Peter Hurkos—has become
internationally famous for his accomplishments in crime
detection, from the finding of mislaid documents or kid-
naped children to the locating of a gang of thieves or the
solving of a brutal murder. Many magazine articles have
been written about him; the Alcoa Hour on television
twice featured his life story; and his autobiography has
recently been published.[7]

3 Psychometry: a term coined about 100 years ago by an American physician, Dr. Buchanan. It refers to the capacity to hold an object in the
hand and to receive vivid impressions concerning its owner and past history.
4 Discussed under the name of Lotte Plaat (her name by a previous marriage) in Encyclopedia of Psychic Science, Nandor Fodor (Arthurs Press,
London, 1933).
5 In My Mind's Eye, Frederick Marion (Wehman Bros., N.Y.).
6 "The World's Most Unusual Detective," True magazine (Jan., 1956).
7 Psychic, The Story of Peter Hurkos (Bobbs-Merrill, 1961).

In 1943 Peter Hurkos fell thirty feet from a ladder while painting a barracks building. He fell on his head and he fractured his skull. When he regained consciousness in the Hague's Zuidwal Hospital he discovered that he unaccountably knew things about other people that were not apparent to his normal five senses.[8]

He told a hospital nurse whom he had never seen before: "Be careful. You may lose a valise that belongs to a friend of yours." She looked at him in amazement: she had just returned from Amsterdam on the train and she had forgotten a borrowed valise in the dining car. He chided the man in the bed next to him for having been disloyal to his father by selling a valuable keepsake watch his father had left him when he died. The man was thunderstruck; he had indeed done that very thing.

Hurkos was, of course, considerably bewildered by what had happened to him. He confided in a close friend, a public accountant named Theo Burger, who tried to help him analyze the way his strange gift worked and to explore its potentials. They found that Burger could sit at the wheel of a car and Hurkos, blindfolded, could sit by his side and predict traffic ahead. Burger would give him photographs of people unknown to both of them, challenging him to tell if the persons were living or dead. On checking later, they found his accuracy was close to 100 per cent. Little by little word spread of his amazing gift and people began to

[8] It is worth noting, perhaps, that there have been a number of instances in which a person's psychic faculties appeared for the first time after a severe fall. These include Edgar Cayce, Ronald Edwin (See *Clock Without Hands*, Ronald Edwin, The Falcon's Wing Press, 1956), and Eusapia Palladino.

come to him for private consultation. Before long he was retained by several industrial firms, including a pulp paper manufacturing plant and a large commercial laundry, to check on personnel and equipment. His job was to take regular inspection trips through the plant; merely by placing his hand over machinery he could sense which part needed replacement and where a motor was about to break down.

But the most dramatic of his accomplishments was in the realm of crime detection, and among the many crimes he was able to solve perhaps the most striking is the case of the series of fires that terrorized a Dutch farming community near Nijmegen in August of 1951.

The holocaust was known to be the work of an arsonist, because the odor of kerosene was discernible in every fire. Four blazes had already been set, at an estimated total damage of about $375,000. Farmers patrolled their fields at night, afraid to go to bed. No one knew which farm would be victimized next.

Late one evening Hurkos and an old friend were hiking across a wheat field. Hurkos was on a visit from a town 40 miles to the north. As they passed the charred remains of a barn Hurkos suddenly received a vivid psychic impression. "There will be another fire set tonight," he said. "I believe it will be the Janson farm. Do you recognize the name?" His friend did. "Let's go to the police department to warn them," the friend suggested.

When they reached the Nijmegen police headquarters and delivered their message, the police chief replied coldly, "I see news travels fast. We got the alarm half an hour ago." Hurkos tried to make clear that he had never heard of the Jansons before, that his knowledge of the fire was due to a strong psychic impression, and that perhaps he could help them discover the arsonist. The police chief was disdainful. Hurkos proceeded to tell him exactly what was in his—the police chief's—trouser pocket with such accuracy that the chief was finally convinced that Hurkos did, indeed, have some supernormal gift. With official permission, then, Hurkos proceeded to search for what he called a "contact." He was taken to each of the farms which had been set fire to thus far, and hunted around in the rubble. Finally he found a small screwdriver, which he held in his hand thoughtfully for some moments. "It's a boy we must look for," he said at last.

Requesting to see the photographs of all the boys of the community, Hurkos was shown school yearbooks, photographers' collections, and police identification files. Finally Hurkos saw the picture that he wanted. "This is your boy!" he exclaimed. The officers were shocked to see that he was pointing to the photograph of the 17-year-old son of one of the wealthiest citizens of Nijmegen.

Hurkos insisted that this was indeed the guilty party. "You'll find him wearing blue overalls. He has a box of matches in one pocket and some lighter fluid in the other." Detectives found the young man in the family garage, wearing blue overalls as Hurkos had said and with matches and lighting fluid in his pockets. At headquarters the boy denied any knowledge of the fires; but when Hurkos said, "You have some deep scratches in your leg, don't you? You got them from the barbed wire of the fence as you were running from the scene of the fire. Pull up your trousers and let us see." Slowly the boy obeyed. His leg was scratched from calf to thigh with angry red scratches. "I can't lie to you," he whispered in fright, and then he made a full confession. Not long afterward the boy was committed to a mental institution.

Hurkos has since come to the United States of America to live. For some time he was in the employ of the Miami, Florida, police department, and a number of crimes in this country have been solved through his psychic faculty. Currently (1963) he makes his home in a small town in Wisconsin, and he has recently been instrumental in the discovery of the location of oil wells and gold deposits.

Here, then, is one area—that of crime detection—in which the very real usefulness of clairvoyance has been dramatically proven. But there are several other areas of human concern which have also been systematically reached by clairvoyant faculty.

Psychotherapy is one such area. I have personally known and studied two sensitives whose work falls predominantly into this category inasmuch as it is of psychological benefit to those who consult them. They are Gladys Valentine Jones and Betty McCain, both of California.

Gladys Valentine Jones is a tall, gracious, unassuming woman whose gift seems to have come as a result of many years of disciplined meditation. It is quite different in character from that of Peter Hurkos. She seems to be incapable, for example, of the type of pin-pointed information that Hurkos can give, on the strength of which a crime can be solved or an oil well located. Whether this is due to actual lack of capacity to reach such matters, or to a profound lack of interest in purely material concerns, I do not know. In any case she is at her best with problems of a more personal nature.

One of the most amazing things she can do is this: given only the name of an individual known to her client, she will proceed to give a description of his general appearance, character, and temperament, and the nature of his relationship to her client.

Another unusual aspect of her gift is the capacity to see a person's life situation in symbolical terms. This is the image she saw for one woman who came to her for consultation:

"I see you living, as it were, on the seashore. From where you are you can see men struggling desperately in the waters of the ocean. You rescue them; lead them to a warm fire which you keep burning; give them food and drink; comfort them; let them talk out their hearts and souls. They seem to have known no other woman like you. Yet after they have regained their strength they grow restless and begin to wonder what is to be found in the green fields above the shore. So before long they leave, one by one, and you remain, alone and lonely, on the sand." The woman acknowledged that this was an accurate representation of her life and her relationship to men.

"You seem to have gotten the essence of everything I've ever experienced," was the comment of one girl, a graduate student in social work at the University of Southern California. The comment is typical of many who consult

Miss Jones. Without the need for ink-blot tests, dream analyses, personality inventories, or any other of the ingenious technical devices of modern psychotherapy, she goes instantly to the very core of a personality, to the very heart of a complicated problem.

Perhaps the most appropriate label for Gladys Jones would be seer, or seeress, to revive an ancient but really rather apt descriptive word. She not only sees the inner reality of a person, but she sees the *meaning* of the job, the illness, the accident, the mother, the friend, the husband, and the purpose of a life experience in an educative sense. People leave her therefore not only with verifiable data— evidential items that would satisfy the exacting criteria of a parapsychologist—but also, for the most part, with a sense of comfort, of perspective, and of insight; something which answers the agonized question: Why did I need to undergo this experience? or the anxious concern: What am I supposed to be doing with my life? These matters are usually unverifiable in a strict evidential sense; but they make possible a renewal of the spirit and hence they have pragmatic and therapeutic value at least.

The second clairvoyant I know whose work is of psychotherapeutic usefulness is Elizabeth or, as she prefers to call herself, Betty McCain. Mrs. McCain is a forthright and direct little person with extraordinary powers of endurance and an intense dedication to her work. As a child she had some intimations of psychic faculty, but it was not until the early 1950's that it developed into a sustained and useful tool.

As in the case of Gladys Jones, Betty McCain's work

does not deal with material matters such as finances, property, lost articles, or crime. It consists rather of therapeutic counsel based on an analysis of a person's temperament, character, talents, and personal relationships. This faculty has been of great help to many people if I may judge from their personal accounts and letters to me, and from the fact that several practicing psychologists and psychiatrists frequently send patients to her for a reading, having found that her clairvoyant insights parallel and supplement their own clinical work.

On a trip through the United States a few years ago, Mrs. McCain stopped in Kansas City, Missouri, and gave some readings. A psychiatrist of that town afterwards wrote me as follows: "I had an opportunity to sit in on an extensive series of readings a very considerable number of which were patients, ex-patients, or persons about whom I had a great deal of information. The results in some instances were quite astonishing. I'm sure that she gave information which could not be simply a lucky guess. The number of details, and the percentage of accuracy, were far too high for a lucky accident. She frequently gave correct details and backgrounds on problems she could not have known about."

Like Edgar Cayce, Mrs. McCain is able to give readings at a distance. Given only a name, an address, and the hour when the individual is likely to be present at that address, Mrs. McCain can direct her Psyche, as she calls it, to that particular spot on the globe, and within several minutes makes the contact that she needs. Then she proceeds to "tune in" to the Psyche of the other person and to relate what she sees just as if the person were present in the room. Actually, it seems as if she is translating into speech as much what she *feels* as what she sees, for in relating emotionally charged experiences she seems to be herself experiencing the grief or terror or joy of the other. The whole process seems to represent, therefore, as much a kind of intensely felt empathy on her part as a perception.

This capacity to read at a distance is of importance because it refutes one of the major objections of skeptics, namely, that all so-called psychic readings are merely clever appraisals based on sensory clues.

In March of 1957 when I first learned of Mrs. McCain's abilities in this direction, I tested her by giving her the name and address of a person well known to me and totally unknown to her, who lives about 1800 miles away from Mrs. McCain's residence. Three questions were asked, the first one being: "Please analyze this person's situation and suggest what can be done to improve it," and the other two questions being equally general and providing no clues to the individual's personality or style of life. Yet in a five-page, single-spaced typewritten transcript of the tape-recorded reading there were by careful count 53 correct items of specific characterization and 6 incorrect ones—which seemed to me to be an extraordinary performance.

In the years since then I have seen a comparable degree of accuracy in many other distance readings, and I have perhaps several dozen letters in my files, including one from Japan and one from Holland, testifying to this fact. However, I do not wish to give the impression that all persons for whom she has read are helped by the reading or that Mrs. McCain's accuracy is infallible. On the contrary, I have seen many instances in which her reading has been far from accurate and the subject has been far from pleased. Rather like the famous little girl who had a little curl, right in the middle of her forehead; and when she was good she was very very good, and when she was bad she was horrid, when Mrs. McCain is good, she is very very good; and when she is bad, she is extremely disappointing. It might be said, in fact, that her work ranges on a scale from superlative down through mediocre and at times very poor. Her readings have a tendency to be wordy and repetitious and her own very positive and forceful, not to say peppery, personality sometimes seems to alienate people and to militate against the establishment of a good rapport.

It is for reasons such as these that I am always hesitant to recommend any psychic, including Mrs. McCain, because it is impossible for me to guarantee performance. Fluctuations of faculty are characteristic of all clairvoyants. This is true of Peter Hurkos and of Gladys Jones, and it was also true of Edgar Cayce, though some of his followers are perturbed to hear it.

Obviously if a person has only one contact with a psychic and this happens to be on an "off" day when, due to bad rapport, physical indisposition, or other reasons, performance is not very good, that person is likely to go away with the impression that clairvoyance is nothing but a farce and the individual in question is only a fraud. But such a conclusion is both unfair and unscientific. A psychic deserves at least as much careful consideration as a hypothesis, and any person who presumes to pass judgment on the person, or on the whole field, has a moral and scientific obligation to be thorough in his examination.

Persons who *are* thorough in their study cannot fail to come to the realization that clairvoyance is a very real thing and that it is indeed an important way of gaining knowledge—knowledge that is often inaccessible otherwise, or accessible only with much laborious and time-consuming effort. Someone has remarked: "The man who denies the fact of clairvoyance is not entitled to be called a skeptic; he is merely ignorant." I do not think this overstates the case.

But a fair, objective, and thorough investigation of a clairvoyant is not enough. It is of equal importance that the investigator, once convinced, does not thereafter lose sight of the very real limitations of clairvoyance and of the fact that the persons who are the human instruments of this methodology are not dependable in the same way that a microscope or a telescope is. Some of the most important of these limitations may be listed as follows.

1) Clairvoyants are not infallible. An average of 85 per cent accuracy is extraordinarily high. If this seems disappointing, remember that physicians, surgeons, and psychologists are not infallible either, however great their integrity or their professional excellence. And even huge analogue and digital computers have been known to make mistakes. In view of this fallibility, then, it is unwise to follow clairvoyant advice too slavishly or uncritically in crucial matters. Sometimes it is advisable to get legal, medical, or other expert information to supplement, confirm,

or qualify psychic counsel. I have known several persons who did not take this precaution, and who as a result became involved in extremely costly business ventures or in very awkward personal predicaments. These could have been avoided, in one case, by a conversation with a person familiar with the publishing business, and in another case by a simple item of legal information.

2) Clairvoyants are not omniscient. Just because they can see areas unavailable to normal sight does not mean they can see everything about all things. "If she's such a good clairvoyant, why does she ask me what's the price of fish?" a clerk in a market once remarked contemptuously. He was assuming, as many people do, that all levels of reality are accessible to a psychic, including all the everyday trivia of life. This is a mistaken assumption. A psychic does not go about in a psychic state all the time. It would probably drive him insane if he did. It requires, usually, an act of will to "tune in" on something or somebody, and unless there is some good reason for doing so a psychic would not waste his energies in trying to determine, psychically, the price of fish if he could easily find it out in a normal manner. Moreover, though a good psychic has his gift under control, so to speak, as compared to persons who only get occasional flashes of psychic perception, it is not *completely* under control and he cannot always "see" everything he wants to.

Another important consideration is this: some psychics function best on a material level, dealing with crime detection, for example; others on a psychological level; others on a medical level. Very few function equally well

on all. There is specialization of faculty even among clairvoyants, which is not unnatural; we do not go to a criminal
lawyer on a civil case, nor do we expect a pastry cook to be
good at making salads.

3) Clairvoyants are observers and interpreters of life, as
we all are, differing from the rest of us only in that they
have a wider range of vision in space and time. They are
subject, therefore, to the same, or at least similar, difficulties as any observer and interpreter. Inescapably they see
things from their own special point of view, through the
filter of their own mind, personality, and experience, in
the perspective of their own philosophy of life. Sometimes
they see in symbols, and misinterpret the symbol which
they see. Frequently they cannnot distinguish between a
future fact and a future possibility. Often they confuse a
powerfully held thought with an objective reality.

4) The work of clairvoyants, like that of artists, crafts-
men, and professional people generally, varies in excellence from month to month, from day to day, even from
hour to hour, depending on many mental, physical, and
psychological factors. Even a housewife does not have absolutely uniform successes with her pies and her roasts.
Sometimes a clairvoyant does exceptionally accurate and
penetrating work; sometimes he does not. Moreover, the
gifts of a psychic, like those of a singer, may be subject to
gradual deterioration with illness, advancing age, or other
physical and psychological factors.

5) The effectiveness of a clairvoyant, like that of a
psychotherapist, depends in large part on the rapport
between him and the other person. Any personal antago-

nism or even mild dislike which is felt on either side is
bound to affect adversely the efforts of the psychic. Strong
skepticism and a belligerent "show me" attitude is particularly detrimental.

6) Clairvoyants are human beings with human limitations. They have their quota of normal human frailties
and normal human problems, domestic and financial, but
they also have the additional stresses and strains imposed
on them by their peculiar type of work. Many people
naïvely suppose that gifts of this type can belong only to
"spiritual," superior, and godlike beings. Nothing could
be further from the truth. It is no doubt true that the
purer the channel, the more accurate and profound the
psychic vision; but at the present stage of human history
on this planet, pure and perfect channels are exceedingly
rare. If you consult a clairvoyant, therefore, you must
remember that you are consulting a person with a special
talent, nothing more. He may smoke, drink, eat meat,
indulge immoderately in sweets, or do many other things
which do not fit into your preconceived picture of what a
clairvoyant should be.

Anyone who goes to a well-recommended clairvoyant,
then, either out of scientific curiosity or for consultation
on a personal problem, must take all these factors into
consideration, or he is going with unrealistic expectations.

At the outset of this discussion I remarked that, as far as
most people are concerned, trying to demonstrate the possibility of reincarnation on the basis of clairvoyance is

rather like trying to prove the existence of a pixie on the testimony of a leprechaun.

Once it is recognized, however, that clairvoyance is a true faculty of the human mind, the situation becomes considerably different. Now we are trying to prove the existence of a pixie, so to speak, not on the testimony of a nonexistent leprechaun, but on the testimony of a man. . . .

The task is still not easy. In fact, it is studded with difficulties. But at least it comes more within the range of the feasible than it did before.

Suppose we are walking down a country lane with a friend, who is a professor of botany at the state university. All at once he stops short, stares fixedly at the foot of an elm tree, and says: "Good heavens! There's a pixie underneath that elm!" We look at him askance, wondering if he has suddenly lost his mind. But, all absorbed, and looking steadily at the same spot, he begins to describe the pixie in some detail—its features, its clothing, its movements; and he does so with the same careful precision, the same authoritative manner, that marks his professional description of plants and flowers. We are likely to be confounded, but not convinced.

Suppose, further, that over a period of years every time we visit our friend the professor at his home in the suburbs, he continues to describe the pixies that he sees, and his descriptions are always consistent with each other and plausible in the light of the laws of nature that we know. Suppose too that he continues to do competent and even brilliant work in his own professional field, and we know him to be of eminently sound mind and of unimpeachable moral character and honesty. Suppose still further that, having become intrigued by the subject, we have investigated elsewhere and have learned that other botanists and zoologists in other parts of the world, unknown to our friend and unknown to each other, have also been describing pixies lately, and that their descriptions not only tally with each other, but with ancient traditions handed down in the religions of the East. All of them say that the painting of violets and the designing of pansy faces are under the direction of pixies, and all of them say that pixies stand about twelve inches tall, have the warm brown complexions of a Mexican, and usually wear a green pointed cap with a feather in it. . . .

At this point we begin to realize that perhaps pixies are not as preposterous, and our friend the botanist not as daft, as we may have originally thought.

Let us drop our fable and go back to the facts.

Suppose we have discovered a clairvoyant named Edgar Cayce, whose work we study for a long period of time. We find that his statements, when checked, show a high percentage of accuracy. He has made several thousand correct statements about things remote from him in space and time, unknowable to him by normal means. Then— as much to his own surprise as anybody else's—he suddenly begins to see and talk about reincarnation. He talks earnestly, coherently, consistently, in considerable detail, with irreproachable logic, and with a quiet air of authority. Shall we believe him, or not?

Many people, confronted with this inevitable question, have answered it with a flat and uncompromising *No*. "Cayce's physical readings were wonderful," they say, "but I can't accept his life readings." It is difficult to see how they can draw so neat and absolute a line. Their rejection of the reincarnation aspects of his work almost seems to be indicative of a philosophic position already firmly fixed. On the other hand, a prompt and unqualified *Yes* might be too generous an answer. For my part, I have after due deliberation answered the question with a tentative and qualified *Yes*.

I say qualified, because the limitations of clairvoyance are what they are. Let me repeat them: clairvoyants may have a high percentage of accuracy but they are not infallible; they are not omniscient; they see things through the filter of their own mind and personality; their work fluctuates in excellence and it is dependent on the rapport between themselves and the other person. *If these limitations prevail when clairvoyants are dealing with the realm of the normally knowable, these limitations must also prevail when clairvoyants are dealing with the realm of the normally unknowable.* Hence I have the feeling that there may well be errors and distortions in the readings of Cayce as regards past lives—how frequent the errors or how large the distortions I have no way of knowing, and only future research can establish it.

In the meanwhile, I also feel that the past-life information that he gave, both as regards individuals and as regards the general laws under which karma operates, have a certain general validity. I have this confidence because of reasons more fully outlined elsewhere,[9] but I may say briefly here that the past-life data had sufficient points of anchorage, so to speak, with confirmable truth, as to bring conviction to me in my survey.

There are those who dismiss all the past-life information as a mere fantasy production—a dramatic superstructure built upon some fragment of psychological truth. I do not doubt at all that this may sometimes happen. I am not here referring to deliberate and unprincipled fraud, a matter which I shall discuss in the next chapter. I am referring rather to a creative mechanism of the mind. One need only make a study of dreams to discover how inventive the mind can be—how agile, how ingenious, how fertile—once the firm hold of the conscious mind is relaxed. Most of us know from firsthand experience how a small physical discomfort such as the tangling of a sheet around one foot will give rise to an elaborate and dramatic dream story involving a trapped foot. By analogy we might be able to assume that a good psychic—accurately picking up a trait of character in another person, such as a love of study and seclusion, could then create an elaborate story set in the Middle Ages in which that person was a monk in a monastery, all the details of the episode being provided by nothing but creative imagination.

This may well happen at times but I cannot believe that it always happens, because, for one thing, sometimes the story can in part at least be objectively confirmed.

For example: Cayce once gave a reading on a blind man,

[9] See *Many Mansions,* Chapter 3.

a musician by profession, who regained part of his vision in one eye through following the physical suggestions given by Cayce. This man happened to have a passion for railroads and a tremendous interest in the Civil War. In the life reading which Cayce gave, he said that the man had been a soldier in the South, in the army of Lee, and that he had been a railroad man by profession in that incarnation. Then he proceeded to tell him that his name in that life was Barnett Seay, and that the records of Seay could still be found in the state of Virginia. The man took the trouble to hunt for the records—and found them, in the state capitol at Richmond: that is to say, he found the record of one Barnett Seay, standard-bearer in Lee's army, who had entered and been discharged from the service in such and such a year.

It is difficult to maintain, I think, that this was all a mere fantasy on Cayce's part when we are confronted with this piece of tangible confirmation. To explain it away one would need to assume an act of clairvoyant perception to pick up the man's interests, temperament, and character; plus a creative fantasy on the basis of this perception; plus a separate act of clairvoyance to pick up an existing and findable registry in Virginia; plus a quick act of assembly to make of it all a kind of pasted-up montage. This, of course, is still not beyond the range of possibility; but to me it seems implausible.

In short, my position on the question of creative fantasy is that it is not impossible; that it may have occasionally happened with Cayce on his "off" days but that it did not happen with regularity; and that it may well happen with greater frequency with other psychics of lesser capacity than Cayce's. My rule of thumb has been this: If a clairvoyant shows 85-90 per cent accuracy in his contact with checkable reality, then in all probability he is contacting uncheckable reality with 85-90 per cent accuracy also. Another subsidiary rule of thumb has been: The purer the life of the clairvoyant, the freer his nature from personality blocks and ego drives, the more likely is his vision to be undistorted, especially as regards psychological and spiritual matters.

These have been my underlying assumptions, and they may be mistaken ones. But I am reassured by the fact—as I indicated in my little fable—that there are other botanists seeing pixies and describing them in the same way. By this I mean that the data of age-regression hypnosis, the data of other clairvoyants, the data of spontaneous past-life recall, the visionary experiences of LSD, and the ancient traditions of Hinduism and of yogic thought, all seem to confirm and substantiate each other as to the general principles under which reincarnation operates. The Cayce data showed, for example, that it is not uncommon for souls, even well-evolved souls, to return to incarnation in a relatively short period of time, such as a year, two years, five years, or twenty years, despite a Theosophical tradition to the contrary. Age-regression experiments have independently confirmed this, as have the spontaneous memory cases studied by Dr. Stevenson, and the work of other clairvoyants who touch on past lives.

Clairvoyance may not, in the last analysis, prove to be the best single means of demonstrating the reality of reincarnation, just as the exclamation: "I see a pixie!" will probably long remain a matter of dubious truth to anybody who cannot see pixies for himself. But clairvoyance may prove to be the best single means of directing attention to the areas where manifestations of reincarnation may be found. Then, using other and perhaps more precise instruments of knowledge, investigators may be able to corroborate, enlarge on, and finally prove with scientific rigor what clairvoyance has led the way to.

The day of proof will be a momentous day in the history of mankind.

3

A FEW WORDS FRANKLY SPOKEN
Reincarnation and Modern Psychology

I

Some years ago a university psychologist had in his experimental laboratory a very intelligent chimpanzee named Susan. Curious as to whether or not he could teach Susan to play tennis, he took her into the college gymnasium one morning and, hitting the ball against the wall, proceeded to demonstrate to her all his best tennis strokes. Susan sat on the sidelines, her bright brown eyes attentively following his every move. Finally, after about a half an hour of vigorous effort, the psychologist concluded that she had seen enough. Mopping his brow, he placed the racket and the tennis ball carefully on the floor and left the gymnasium. After a brief interval of waiting outside the door, he very quietly raised the opening of the little observation window, wondering if Susan had already begun to experiment with the game. But all that he could see was one small, brown beady eye, looking out at him. . . .

It would seem that, while the psychologist was speculating about Susan's intelligence, she was also secretly wondering about *his*.

I have often thought of this story as I observe the mutual

suspicion with which university psychologists and those fringe groups known as metaphysical or occult usually regard each other. For the most part they simply ignore each other's existence; but when the occasion arises to take some notice, it is apparent that each considers the intelligence of the other to be defective. Like Susan and the psychologist of the story, they find themselves on opposite sides of a wall, through which they peer at each other from time to time with undisguised disdain.

This situation seems to me to be very unfortunate. Like a half-breed, I find myself in the position of belonging partially to both groups and fully to neither. I find myself, therefore, acutely sensitive to the merits and demerits of both. I can clearly see with the university professors those areas of the fuzzy, the foggy, the absurd, the pretentious, the unsubstantiated, and even the fraudulent that exist in the fringe societies. And yet, with the fringe societies, I can see the rigidities, the intolerances, the unexamined assumptions, and the arrogant condescensions of which the university professors are so often guilty. I am unhappy about what I see in both camps, and yet I find much to admire in both. I am convinced that each has something to gain from the other, and I look for the day when the contributions of both can be fused.

One of the areas of respectable psychology which is, in my opinion, in need of considerable modification is that of philosophic assumptions. Materialism is a perfectly proper philosophic position, just as a bustle is a perfectly proper feminine garment. It is just that both of them are considerably out of date. The materialist notion, for example, that only that which can be seen or otherwise apprehended by the senses is real, we now know to be untrue. Yet most psychologists who recognize this fact still exclude the possibility of a soul (which we shall define here, roughly, as that living thing which leaves the body at death and continues to exist elsewhere) precisely because nobody has ever seen one.

"Is there anybody here who thinks he has a soul?" a psychology professor in a certain state university asked recently. "If so, please park it outside before you come into this classroom." The remark was greeted with laughter, and the attitude it represents is typical of perhaps 95 per cent of psychologists and psychoanalysts in America. The soul is something for which they, together with most intellectuals of our time, feel only amused contempt.

Historically this is of course understandable. The soul has been associated in Christian tradition with a monstrously incredible theological system, and with a world view filled with superstition and prescientific assumptions. And scientifically it is also understandable. Science deals only with that which can be seen, or, if not seeable, that which can be otherwise measured.

But a percipient student of history and religion must realize that many times true ideas degenerate and become repellent because of their association with false ones, or because their acceptance has been forced upon us by stupid and venal men, for their own advantage. And an up-to-date student of science surely must know that visibility is no criterion of actuality. No one has ever seen an atom; its existence is known only by inference. And so new methods of studying and measuring may be required for dealing with realities hitherto unknown to us.

It might therefore be wise not to assume too dogmatically that a soul is nothing but a superstition and that the long-persistent legend about its continuance after death could have no possible foundation in fact. But it is this rigid assumption with which most psychologists approach not only the soul's existence and continuance, but also its possible evolution through a reincarnatory process.

So rigid, indeed, are these psychologists' materialistic and mechanistic assumptions, that even when they are confronted with minor but nonetheless significant inferential evidences, small straws in the wind, pointing in the direction of something nonmaterial, they regard them for the most part with contempt, and reduce them to the dimensions of their own Procrustean bed. This attitude was particularly in evidence when the Bridey Murphy case came forcibly to their attention some years ago, and it is still apparent, not only among the practitioners of the psychological professions themselves, but among thousands of otherwise intelligent people whose minds have been unduly influenced by their psychoanalysts and by a widespread psychological literature of materialist persuasion.

It used to be in Christian countries that reincarnationists were regarded as heretics, and if they were vocal about their belief they were likely to be burned at the stake. But little by little Christians became somewhat less bloodthirsty, and in recent times a person who has admitted to a belief in reincarnation has merely been regarded as a credulous crackpot.

But that was before the era of psychoanalytical sophistication. Now the disparagement and the insults go underground, so to speak, and the reincarnationist is clinically
dissected for his unconscious motivations. "It's only natural
for him to believe in reincarnation," someone said disdain-
fully in my hearing concerning a man we both knew. "He's
a cripple." This is typical of the new approach.

There are two major implications in this remark.

The first is that people believe in reincarnation because
they have some serious deficiency in their body or their
life and hence desperately feel the need of another chance.
This fails to take into account those thousands of reincarnationists who have perfectly sound bodies, lead lives of
no greater frustration than anybody else, and accept reincarnation on the sheer force of its logic.

The second implication is that the reincarnation idea
satisfies a psychological need for the continuance of life; it
is a wish fulfillment idea and hence of no account scientifically speaking. There may well be some truth in the idea
that the reincarnation theory does satisfy certain powerful
unconscious wishes; but it has never been clear to me by
what right materialists can assume that their own philosophic position arises from a wishless unconscious—an unconscious of pristine neutrality and purity. It seems never
to have occurred to them that materialism, and the conviction that death ends everything, could well arise from:

1) a deep-seated masochistic pessimism;
2) an unconscious hatred and fear of life; and, hence,
3) the deep wish for its permanent cessation.

Nor has it occurred to them, apparently, that agnosticism could be related to:

1) a deep-seated insecurity as to one's own powers of thought;
2) a basic distrust of the father image due to an early betrayal of trust; and, hence,
3) a deep-seated doubt as to the order and beneficence of the universe.

That psychological uncertainty or negativity should be any more indicative of the nature of reality than psychological affirmativeness or hope is a highly questionable assumption; yet it is widely prevalent among those who pride themselves on their own rigorous objectivity.

The shocking lack of real objectivity within the psychological professions became very conspicuous when the Bridey Murphy story was sweeping the country; and perhaps no more shocking exhibition of it could be found than in a book, hastily issued, called *A Scientific Report on the Search for Bridey Murphy*.[1] The title should properly be placed in quotes because a more unscientific book could scarcely be imagined.

The book was a symposium, edited by Milton V. Kline, Ph.D., in which a group of psychiatrists and psychoanalysts held forth in a manner reminiscent of politicians who, instead of meeting squarely the arguments of their opponent, proceed instead to defame his character.

In the Editor's Foreword, Dr. Kline immediately established the keynote of the book. On page 3, in fact, he said:

1 (The Julian Press, 1956).

"Bridey Murphy as a fantasy of reincarnation is relatively unimportant." The learned authors who followed him did not trouble to examine rigorously any of the many substantiated items of obscure Irish history that were brought up in the Bridey Murphy recall, nor did they give any genuine accounting for them in the mind of an average unscholarly Colorado housewife. But they did not feel that this was necessary, since they knew to begin with that the whole thing was only a fantasy. With Olympian disregard of all verified items, they spent their time instead, and a good deal of psychoanalytical verbiage, in dissecting Morey Bernstein's shortcomings of character and unconscious motivations.

One of the contributors found that Morey had a preoccupation with death and a need for omnipotence, "which might be considered to spring out of his sense of weakness in relation to the father figures in his life" and which "may well lie behind his eagerness to be a hypnotist who, by definition, has almost unlimited power over the life of others." Later this same psychoanalyst suggested that "The Search for Bridey Murphy seems to be an appendix to The Search for Father Bernstein or Father God," and also that "Morey Bernstein's interest in hypnosis and reincarnation is an expression of his hidden rebellion against his father." At still another point she observed that "Morey, it would seem, wishes to experience the 'blissful sea' through a telepathic, hypnotic oneness with (and within?) a Bridey floating in an astral world. This may well be the real motive of his experimentation . . ." [2]

2 Pp. 89, 91, 101, 92.

These astonishing irrelevancies to the real point at issue were written by a "practicing psychoanalyst who uses hypnosis with humility and care"; and the whole volume seldom rises above the same level of complacent inconsequentiality.

To evaluate a man's scientific efforts merely by making a Freudian analysis of his unconscious motivations is not only unscientific; it is also absurd. Perhaps the full absurdity of the procedure can be more clearly appreciated if we project ourselves backward in time and see what Freudians like Dr. Kline and company would have said had they been around when Columbus challenged the authority of the Pope, the Church, the Inquisition, the Bible, the Universities, the State, the crowned heads of Europe, and all right-thinking people everywhere, by affirming that the world was round.

Neglecting of course to examine any of the objective reasons that supported Columbus' point of view—which they would have doubtless referred to as the "round-world fantasy"—they would have probably pointed out that the reason for Columbus' aberration was perfectly clear. Columbus hated his father. Therefore he hated the father-image as represented by the Pope, the Bible, the Church, etc., etc., etc., and naturally felt a compulsion to unseat their authority by denying the obvious truth, which any simpleton could see, that the world was flat.

At the same time, having a fixation on his mother, and more particularly the breast of the mother (being fixated at the oral period) it was only natural that he would see the world as being breast-shaped, or round. The desire to explore the fantasied "round" world was merely a sublimation of his *real* desire, which was, obviously, to know his mother sexually. . . . And water being obviously representative in his unconscious of the amniotic fluid of the mother, the desire to sail his ship through strange but fiercely attractive waters was clearly indicative of his desire to return to the womb.

With these and other similarly dank lucubrations, more indicative of their own prurient preoccupations than of anything in the objective world, they would have felt that they had permanently disposed of the poppycock Columbus was proposing; and they would have proceeded to direct their attention to other, and more important, aberrations of their time.

To be sure, there could have been an infinitesimal particle of truth in what they said—which is the unfortunate thing about much psychoanalytical nonsense. Maybe the nonconformity of Columbus' personality *was* due to a rebellion against the parental figure. Maybe this *was* the psychological spur for his investigative impulse and his daring courage to test his theory against all opposition. But whatever the unconscious origins of his behavior or whatever his personality dynamics, they are completely irrelevant to the validity of his theory, namely, the roundness of the planet.

The same consideration holds true for Morey Bernstein or anybody else who is attracted to the reincarnation theory, including the cripple who wants another chance in life. Perhaps a cripple in his frustration *does* take more interest in the mysteries of life and death than does a normal person; but this does not, therefore, discount the results of his investigation if he reaches them with thoroughness and objectivity, and if other persons, investigating the matter independently and having *other* deplorable unconscious motivations, come out with the same result.

Certainly there are unconscious motivations present in all of us; but I fail to see why it is only the idealists and the reincarnationists who must be considered guilty of it and why all others, especially the materialist psychoanalysts and the anti-reincarnationists should consider themselves exempt. In fact, the more I consider the matter, the more I am inclined to feel that there may well be—in those cases where the opposition is not due to sheer ignorance of what the theory really means—some powerful unconscious motivations operative in anti-reincarnationists, and particularly in rabid anti-reincarnationists.

It is significant, I think, that the theory of reincarnation and karma is one of uncompromising accountability and responsibility. Could it possibly be that people who bitterly oppose it are people who must have someone else to blame (Adam, if they are orthodox Christians; their parents, if they are orthodox behaviorists) for their condition? Could it possibly be that people who violently attack a theory which requires the transformation of the self by the self are people who must have someone else (Jesus or the psychoanalyst) to save them from their own folly? Could it be that people who find the reincarnation idea fantastic, ridiculous, and repulsive are people who have an undeveloped sense of moral responsibility or an imperfect sense of integrity and honesty? people who want something for nothing in life? essentially immature people?

I do not mean to suggest that these are the only reasons for rejecting the reincarnation idea; I am sure there are many other reasons, both conscious and unconscious. But I am saying that these are some possible reasons for it— just as possible as that a reincarnationist should be that way because he happens to hate his father, be a cripple, or have a deep unconscious wish for another chance in life.

I am also saying that psychoanalytical mudslinging is a game that everyone can play, if necessary; but it hardly comes to grips with the objective and important facts at issue.

Members of the psychological professions and all other patronizing critics of reincarnation would do well therefore to do a little self-examination and a little examination of their own unconscious assumptions before publicly condemning something about which they have not taken the trouble to inform themselves well.

The attitude of the psychological professions towards reincarnation is one area which calls for improvement. I am not saying this only because I would like to see them accept reincarnation, though such an acceptance would undoubtedly add a new dimension to psychology and give both precision and depth to many aspects of psychological theory. I am saying it also because their behavior with regard to it, one sample of which I have just referred to, is indicative of a smug habit of mind, a set of unexamined and completely outdated metaphysical assumptions, a lack of alertness in the presence of possible new knowledge, and a general rigidity of mind which they would quickly recognize in a patient as symptomatic of some kind of immaturity.

We are in too serious a global emergency for our very psychologists to be unaware, unalert, and uninformed regarding *anything* that can be of help to mankind. Even if reincarnation is finally proven to be indeed a fantasy and a delusion, what if some other, true, theory, some major breakthrough in the psychological field, should appear? Would not the behavior of the psychiatrists and psychoanalysts be just as rigid, just as obstructive, as it has been in the case of Bernstein's Bridey Murphy? This is my essential point.

II

On the other hand, there is and has been much in the occult field in general and the reincarnation field in particular which also bears improving.

If academic psychologists have almost universally erred in their excess of materialist skepticism, the unacademic occultists and metaphysicians have all too often erred in their excess of credulity.

I am not referring here to those crackpottish misfits, some of them borderline psychotics, who have been attracted to the unorthodox societies of our times and who are conspicuously lacking in good judgment and good sense. There is a small minority of people of this type; but they have always existed and if they had not attached themselves to the esoteric societies they would have attached themselves to anything else that gave them refuge and comfort.

I am referring rather to those people who are not obviously or eccentrically neurotic, who may or may not have had some college education, who are literate, reasonably intelligent, and studious, and who, because of life problems for which they found no answers or solutions elsewhere, have gone into the more offbeat religious and philosophic groups. I include members of such societies as Theosophy; the Rosicrucian order; the Anthroposophical Society of Rudolf Steiner; the Association for Research and Enlightenment, which studies Edgar Cayce's work; and even such groups as the Unity School of Christianity and Religious Science, whose primary emphasis is on religious and practical techniques of living.

In the membership of these groups one finds many earnest and studious people and most of them sincerely try to live their life by a philosophy which has been of their own choosing. As individuals and as representatives of their respective groups they have, I feel, a definite contribution to make to society; and what I say here is said only because I would wish them to be less gullible in certain matters and, therefore, less open to the ridicule of the academically trained.

One of the most recent manifestations of this gullibility has been precisely in the area of reincarnation. Ever since the Edgar Cayce material and the Bridey Murphy case came to public attention, there has been a growing number of persons who have come to believe in the theory. One of the first questions that many of them ask is, "Who could I have been in my past lives?". . . and there has been no dearth of people who are willing to answer the question for a price ranging from $5 to $300. One gentleman, on the basis of the date and place of your birth plus a button from a frequently used garment, will give you a $5 life reading revealing all the talents you have brought over from past lives. An astrologer advertises a horoscope with three retrogressed past lives for $25, each additional incarnation to cost $5. A reader of the Akashic Records[3] explains not only one's karmic relationship to people on earth but also to flying saucer people from other planets. There is even someone who will tell you not only how to awaken the untapped forces within you from your past lives, but also how to plan and control your next incarnation, and find your Soul Mate as well. All these people may conceivably have something of genuine value to offer, but it cannot be accepted blindly or uncritically.

To be sure, I have gone on record as believing in reincarnation and I have devoted a good deal of time, thought, and printed space to the Cayce data on past lives. So it might well seem unbecoming of me to make any sound of protest on the score of past-life readings. But make it I must, because there are certain elements in the situation that need airing and I would feel myself negligent in a self-incurred obligation if I did not do so.

A brief and rather undramatic case history here will

---

3 *Akasha* is a Sanskrit term referring to the fundamental substance of the universe. According to Hindu philosophic thought, there is recorded upon it, as on a sensitive photographic plate, every event since the beginning of the manifest universe; and the capacity of seers to see the past is due to their ability to tune in to this vibratory transcription.

serve to highlight the basic nature of the problem. A woman acquaintance of mine became interested in reincarnation and went to a psychic who advertised past-life readings. She told me with some excitement afterwards that he had revealed to her thirteen of her past lives, and had even given her the names of her husbands in all of those lives . . . I asked her, when she finished her long recital, if he had told her the first name of her current husband, or anything else specific and checkable about her present life, and she said No, he hadn't—but the past lives were so fascinating!

Not one verifiable item about the present did he tell her; yet this woman was willing to believe the man was clairvoyant, just because he advertised himself as such, and to accept the entire romantic tale that he concocted as certain truth. One would think that the merest common sense would point to the need for some minimum proof of his psychic capacity; but apparently this woman, and many others, do not have that much common sense.

It is these two things that I find deplorable: that a glib and unscrupulous person with a fertile imagination, a smattering of occult knowledge, and a readiness to exploit a tide of popular interest should be able to get rich in this manner; and that persons who have intelligence enough to know better should be taken in by it. In this particular case no serious harm was done. The woman was well able to afford the $25 she paid for a 13-part fascinating but dubious romance, though it surely could have been better spent than to enrich a charlatan. To my knowledge she suffered no psychological ill effects from anything the man told her, which, judging from what she told me about it, must have been vapid and superficial throughout. But I know of other cases in which misleading pseudo-information has implanted suggestions in the person's mind that were potentially the source of considerable harm.

It is all very well to believe in clairvoyance and in the possibility of obtaining otherwise inaccessible knowledge in this manner. But the problem is this: there are persons who have some small psychic or intuitive gift who, because of their lack of education, or sometimes because of their sense of self-importance, overestimate their own capacity and regard as absolute truth their highly subjective impressions. And there are other persons who have some small psychic or intuitive gift and who crassly decide to capitalize on it—combining some fragmentary psychic perceptions with a shrewd appraisal of personal appearance, and with these thematic foundations improvising a series of four-, five-, six-, or even thirteen-part inventions.

Unfortunately, the general public has little protection against either of these two types of "psychic." Most cities have ordinances against fortunetelling—laws, incidentally, which indiscriminately penalize genuine psychics as well as fraudulent or partially fraudulent ones—but in many places these ordinances are not strictly enforced and in any case it is always possible to circumvent them.

What is needed, and the need is becoming more and more pressing, is a new and more enlightened legal outlook. There should be laws requiring all psychics to be licensed, but not merely by the simple procedure of paying a yearly fee to the city, as they now do in some places. Like barbers, dentists, masseurs, psychologists, and all others who deal intimately with people's minds and bodies, they should have to pass certain examinations and meet certain professional standards.

The examinations should include questions of ethics and of general information and there should be a practical demonstration of the psychic faculty claimed. Obviously these tests should be devised by persons who are sympathetic to the psychic field, not by those who are hostile and uninformed. In order that the tests will be both rigorous and fair, the persons who administer them should be well acquainted with the tricks and devices of fraudulent or semifraudulent psychics, and also with the inevitable fluctuations of faculty of those who are genuine. In England, I understand, there are already tests of this type, administered not by the Government, but by some Spiritualist alliance for all Spiritualist mediums; and it is certainly a very wise provision.

Frankly, I do not foresee the passing of such laws in the United States very soon. There are too many reactionary pressures from orthodox religion and orthodox psychology to allow for any enlightened legal measures for a number of decades, if then.

But in the meanwhile, the problem remains. The only protection that people have against this kind of exploitation and malpractice must lie in their own discrimination. There are a number of criteria which can and indeed must be applied. They are as follows:

1) Try not to go to a psychic unless he or she is recommended to you by a person whose judgment you trust.

2) Be suspicious of a psychic whose prices are exorbitant. A workman is worthy of his hire and psychics like everyone else in our material civilization must live. But if a person who claims he is reading the Akashic records charges prices ranging above $50 for an hour's service or less, you can be almost certain that he is more interested in the cash in Akasha than in any desire to be of spiritual service to you.

3) Do not believe *anything* a psychic tells you about a past life unless he first tells you something specific, accurate, and checkable about your present life—something already known to you, but which he cannot possibly infer from a shrewd examination of your appearance. Unless he can tell you six to ten such items at the very least, you should be highly dubious of anything else he might say.

4) Be suspicious of a past-life reader who flatters you and tells you you were somebody famous or of great importance in the past. If a supposed past life does not explain some of your present tendencies, weaknesses, or problems, and if it does not give you self-insight and a new sense of direction and purpose, it is utterly worthless, and you can be certain that you have wasted both your time and your money.

5) Do *not* provide a psychic with a great deal of information about yourself. If it is suggested that you ask questions about what you want to know, keep your questions as general as possible and provide as little information as possible. A good psychic does not need to be given detailed

information about you; and if he asks for it, be on your guard.

The tendency to be overly gullible with regard to psychic information on past lives is especially prevalent at the present time due to the current wave of interest in reincarnation. But this specific gullibility is very closely related to another more general and more comprehensive credulity. I refer to the tendency of many members of esoteric groups to believe anything in their particular body of literature merely because it is in print and merely because it was said by the founder of the organization or, in some cases, by some revered successor to the founder.

I have found this credulity in almost every esoteric group with which I have ever been acquainted, and while it is understandable—the human need for certainty being what is is—it is also unfortunate.

Two examples may serve to illustrate the point: the Association for Research and Enlightenment, and the Theosophical Society, based on the work of Edgar Cayce and Helena Petrovna Blavatsky respectively.[4] Both Cayce and Blavatsky were psychics of extraordinary and well-documented capacity. Cayce, whose readings were stenographically recorded and are available for examination by any qualified investigator, made literally hundreds of accurate statements about the physical condition or the psychological nature of people, total strangers, who were

[4] The A.R.E. (as it is referred to) has its headquarters at Virginia Beach, Va. The Theosophical Society has its American headquarters at Wheaton, Ill., and its international headquarters at Adyar, India.

thousands of miles away. Mme. Blavatsky, though much maligned, had a variety of paranormal faculties, witnessed by many creditable people of her time; and her great book, *The Secret Doctrine,* contained technical statements which were laughed at when the book appeared in 1888 but which have since been confirmed by the science of the twentieth century. It is only natural for one who knows of these extraordinary confirmations of both Cayce and Blavatsky to take their material seriously and to regard the as yet unproven parts of it with as much respect as the already proven part. I myself have done so, and—there being of course a distinction between respect and total acceptance —I make no apologies for it.

But—though this will seem like the rankest heresy to some of the members of the two organizations in question —the fact must be squarely faced that *no* psychic, however authentic and however remarkable, is 100 per cent accurate. Human perception is always fallible, and the same holds true of human extrasensory perception. Anybody who has made a close study of the Cayce readings knows that Cayce made mistakes *with regard even to checkable items.* Blavatsky, though a different kind of psychic, was also not infallible. She may well have told the truth, and nothing but the truth, as she saw it in 1886; but we have no license to assume that she told *all* the truth, some of it being inaccessible at the time even to her. Moreover she was, presumably, transmitting information from higher intelligences. How can we be sure that there were no errors of interpretation or of recording on her part?

And so when we consider the unproven part of the work

of both Cayce and Blavatsky, we must realize that we may be dealing with a certain percentage of error. We must also recognize that whatever we accept of the unproven data from their work we are accepting *on faith*. It is not blind faith, to be sure; it is more of a reasoned faith. But it *is* faith, and we must therefore, if we have any intellectual probity at all, be somewhat tentative about it. We must be careful not to regard it as a new and infallible revelation (as far too many of their followers do regard it) but rather *as starting points for speculative thought and, above all, for research,* either by orthodox or unorthodox means, or both.

It is precisely in this respect that so many followers of Cayce and Blavatsky, like the followers of other psychics who have originated present-day movements, have made their greatest mistake. It is precisely at this point that it would be well for them to be better acquainted with the painstaking methods of modern psychology, and above all with the basic philosophy of modern science, which is to regard nothing as truth unless it has been subjected to research and experiment. The day of authority has passed. Those who continue to believe without critical examination what some authority says—even if that authority be the words of an authentic clairvoyant—are not only reverting in spirit to the age of superstition, but they are inviting a new wave of superstition, almost as mischievous as the old.

I cannot recall about whom it was said—Rossini, perhaps?—that he wore his fame, not like a cloak, but like a flower in his buttonhole. The simile is apt. It may not be transposable exactly to the case in point, but it is suggestive. Far too many Cayceites and Theosophists wrap themselves complacently in their special information as in a cloak; and they thereby shut themselves in from the sun and the wind of new insights, as well as frighten away those who might otherwise be attracted to them.

The fault here, as in the case of so many movements and religions, lies not with the originators, but with well-meaning but injudicious followers. Edgar Cayce himself always had doubts as to the veracity of his own work. His son, Hugh Lynn Cayce, who for many years has been the director of the Association for Research and Enlightenment, has consistently taken the position that his father's psychic data should be tested, not swallowed whole. He has stated repeatedly that the ethical and psychological counsel should be tested in the laboratory of everyday living; the medical, historical, and parapsychological material should be tested by other suitable means. But far too many of the Cayce followers, including even some of the leaders of local study groups, close their eyes to this point of view and earnestly go about believing, and teaching, items from the Cayce clairvoyance about which I for one would have some considerable reservations. These people also tend to believe that if Cayce did not speak about something, it cannot be of much importance, and that if Cayce did not sanction something, it cannot be true. They are rather like the orthodox Muslim who believes that nothing can be true which is not to be found in so many words in the Koran.

In the ranks of the Theosophical Society one can witness the same phenomenon. Since its inception in 1875, there have always been intelligent members who have had the same critical temper of mind as characterizes Hugh Lynn Cayce and as characterized Mme. Blavatsky herself. But it is only to be expected that in a Society that has been in existence almost a century there should have been many hundreds of people whose willingness to believe without proof has led them into the paths of intellectual folly. In fact, anyone who is interested in making a study of credulity run rampant, due to an inadequate sense of scientific caution with regard to clairvoyant and presumed clairvoyant data, could find no better or richer field of study than the history of the Theosophical Society.

Convinced of the validity of the Blavatsky clairvoyance, many Theosophists have blindly accepted the statements of other self-styled clairvoyants, both in and out of their ranks, often without any evidential substantiations whatsoever. Persuaded that Blavatsky was in touch with Masters of wisdom (as well she might have been) they have been willing to believe almost anybody who says he is in touch with a Master. There is no wonder that Theosophists have been in ill repute for so long in academic circles; and the unfortunate thing is that the ill repute has kept away many people who might have found, and still could find, much of value in the original teachings.

Academic psychologists, then—and I include in the term psychiatrists, psychoanalysts, and all members of the various psychological professions—who take a casual look at the various esoteric societies can legitimately find much to criticize. Amongst the members they would find a tendency to credulity and a lack of discrimination; amongst the originators, a tendency to make assertions unaccompanied by proof, or unsusceptible of proof in our present stage of knowledge. In groups like the Association for Research and Enlightenment and the Theosophical Society they would not find the commercialism which marks so many offbeat societies of our times; but in many other organizations the profit motive would be exceedingly apparent, as would be self-deluded invention and even deliberate fraud.

On the other hand, if they would only take the time and trouble to take a closer look at these societies and their literature—and do so with a truly open mind—they could find there certain important values. They would find, for example:

1) an acknowledgment of the availability of super-sensible knowledge through extrasensory means. It is in this direction that science is inevitably tending.

2) a recognition of spiritual realities and spiritual goals in life. This is perhaps the greatest single blind spot and deficiency of academic psychology.

3) a sense of an underlying unity beneath the many seemingly disparate aspects of religion, philosophy, physical science, psychology, and parapsychology.

4) a philosophy of purposiveness and a cosmically rather than a culturally based code of ethics.

5) a great deal of unproven information concerning the nature of the universe and of the human being which can become the starting point for research leading possibly to inestimably important new knowledge.

If psychologists would turn their attention in particular to the reincarnation theory they would find, in addition:

1) an explanation for many otherwise unexplained phenomena of man's psychological life: homosexuality, multiple personality, mental aberrations due to possession, etc.

2) a rationale of human suffering and human limitations.

3) an insight into the cause of individual differences.

4) a deepened understanding of the body-mind relationship.

5) an important clue into the dynamics of the unconscious.

On the other hand, members of esoteric societies would do equally well to regard academic psychology with more than just a passing and contemptuous look. They would do well, in fact, to expose themselves to a few semester-long courses in psychology at some college or university, and to the current articles and research reports of some of the psychological journals. They might become impatient with some of the pedestrian articles they read, or the materialistically biased opinions they hear in psychology classes. But they might, if open-minded and attentive, also acquire:

1) a respect for the hard-won knowledge—whatever its limitations—of the various psychological disciplines.

2) a more discriminating attitude toward the printed word and the assertions of self-styled authorities.

3) a sense of the nature of scientific evidence, and, therefore,

4) a realization that knowledge obtained through extrasensory means cannot be accepted blindly, uncritically, *in
toto*, and without caution.

5) a willingness to regard discrepancies between what
they believe from their sources of information and what
other people believe, not as a reason for argument, hostility, and self-righteousness, but as a starting point for
research.

Reincarnationists in particular would do well to under-
take such an exploratory project because, in addition to the
above-mentioned values, they would find much in modern
psychology that would supplement and expand their own
understanding of reincarnation. They would also find areas
of uncertainty, incompleteness, and hollow pretentiousness,
which need only the theoretical background of reincarnation to leap into clarity, order, and sanity; and to be informed on these matters would enable them to be more intelligent spokesmen for reincarnation when the occasion
arises.

This is a period of history when vast chasms exist between men—chasms dividing the East from the West, the
North from the South, the black from the white, the rich
from the poor, the informed from the uninformed, the intellectual from the intuitive.

It is a time, therefore, when the building of bridges

across the chasms, by persons of courage and insight, is urgently needed.

The chasm between the people in psychological circles and those in esoteric or psychic circles is, I think, one in most urgent need of a bridge.

For these two groups of people—despite all the tremendous differences that separate them—have a common preoccupation: the mind and, if I may beg the question, the soul of man. And out of these come all the other issues of life.

4

Reincarnation and Common Sense

I

"People who believe in reincarnation always like to think they were somebody famous in the past."

This cliché, usually followed by: "They all think they were Cleopatra or Napoleon," has become so threadbare that it seems to me about time that something sensible be said on the subject.

In the first place, it should be pointed out that it is no longer fashionable to be the reincarnation of Cleopatra or Napoleon. This may have been prevalent, among believers, and funny, to nonbelievers, in the early 1900's (see, for example, a comic novel called *Bunker Bean,* written in 1913) but as of this date it is definitely passé.

Currently it is far more modish to be Thomas Jefferson or Nefertite (an earlier queen of Egypt). I personally am acquainted with three gentlemen who believe they are the reincarnation of our third President, and four ladies, all of them in California, who are convinced they were Nefertite, though I am told that other states have a representation also. But of reborn Napoleons or Cleopatras, I know not a one, and I would be happy to see those who are bent on ridicule to bring their material up to date. Otherwise people may begin to suspect that their information on the theory is as obsolete as their ridicule.

In the second place, the validity of the charge that people who believe in reincarnation *always* think they had a famous past needs to be challenged. I have never sent out a questionnaire to reincarnationists asking, "Do you believe you were a famous person in a past life?" and therefore I have no statistical data on the matter. But it will soon become apparent to anyone who seriously looks into the question that those who make this sweeping generalization— namely that *all* reincarnationists believe they were a famous personage—can have made no statistical study either. In fact, they cannot even have exercised a minimal amount of accurate observation.

In my own experience I have known what must add up to hundreds of people who have been believers in the theory of reincarnation; but only a small number of them have professed to be somebody famous in a previous existence. Some of them have thought so on the basis of what seemed to me to be fairly good subjective and objective evidences; and their belief as to their former identity would seem inherently ridiculous only to persons who, without examination, consider the whole idea of reincarnation ridiculous. But—granting the reasonability of reincarnation—there is no good reason why people who were famous in the past could not actually *be* re-embodied at the present time, working on their many and various deficiencies of character. And there is no valid reason why sometimes some of them may not have actual flashes of memory, and other corroborating evidences, of their former identity.

On the other hand, I have also known people who believed they were some famous personage in the past on what seemed to me to be very shallow, questionable, or spurious grounds. These people constitute a small minority, I repeat; but they do exist, and it is unfortunate that it is they who become the peg on which a stereotype is hung.

Their unfounded belief may arise from several different factors, separately or in combination. One factor has to do with unconscious motivations, the principal one being, apparently, an oppressive sense of insignificance and frustration in the present. This, however, is a fairly prevalent human sentiment, which manifests in a multitude of ways from malicious gossip on one end of the spectrum to creative art on the other. The principal difference between its manifestations in the simple-minded reincarnationist and in the simple-minded Christian is that the former finds compensation in a past life of glory, and the latter in a future life of glory, at the right side of God.

Another factor leading to the self-deluded belief in past-life grandeur has to do with intellectual limitations, or with the lack of a critical or a scientific sense. People tend to confuse a strong impression, a few coincidences, a dream, or an "intuition," as they like to call it, with absolute truth. A woman, for example, has an unusually vivid dream one night concerning Egypt. In the dream she is wearing a white dress and a blue and gold necklace. Since she now has a white dress and a blue and gold necklace of which she is very fond, and since as a child she was nick-named "Queenie" by her playmates, she concludes that the dream must hold momentous significance and that she really was a queen in Egypt.

A third factor in past-life fame addiction arises from cultural limitations, or limitations of knowledge. Many people who claim a famous past are ignorant of anything but the most popularly known historical facts concerning the personage in question, and sometimes their limited knowledge is mistaken or confused. In this connection, I think of the young man who assured me that he was the reincarnation of Apollo—a curious circumstance indeed, Apollo being a mythological character (unless, of course, some clever archeologist has just discovered that there really was a man, once, named Apollo, which I am inclined to doubt). I think also of a man I know who is convinced that he is the reincarnation of a famous writer of the past century. One time I had occasion to read the biography of the writer in question and I learned that throughout his life-time he was insufferably vain, completely lacking in a sense of humor, and the possessor of various other rather stuffy traits of character. Inasmuch as these attributes would very probably carry over into whatever present incarnation he might be having, it seems unlikely that my acquaintance ever really took a careful look at the heritage he was claim-ing. This confusion of notoriety or fame with intrinsic su-periority is a common confusion, and particularly prevalent among those who claim some past-life personage as their former self.

So there is certainly truth in the accusation that *some*

reincarnationists have idiotic and grandiose notions concerning themselves; but it is *not* the truth to say that all of them do. Moreover, it must be remembered that self-delusion, arising from conscious and unconscious factors similar to those just outlined, is to be found among the followers of all schools of thought, from Christianity to Freudianism. Human folly is human folly. It manifests itself everywhere, within the confines of any philosophical persuasion.

People who approach the matter of past lives with a serious intellectual or therapeutic purpose do not often come upon any erstwhile grandeur. They may in fact be shocked to discover some pretty sordid and disgraceful past-life behavior including such things as murder, robbery, betrayal, prostitution, or fraud; or some very drab, humdrum, and commonplace existences (like that of Bridey Murphy) which were lived apparently for the acquisition of some homely virtue. Such were the findings of psychiatrist Dr. Blanche Baker of San Francisco who, in the last years of her life used a light hypnotic and free association technique in which patients were induced to go back to what seemed to be previous incarnations. The material dredged up was far from glamorous; and, even if one wishes to call it fantasy material, the fact remains that the experiences so relived resulted in some highly successful therapy.

Though the current wave of interest in reincarnation may result in an increasing number of people with superficial notions of past-life glory, it is also giving rise to a very sincere curiosity, both intellectual and personal, about past lives. Once people recognize the philosophic and psychological cogency of the theory, it is only natural that they should begin to wonder who they were in the past; and then the question naturally arises as to how they may discover their past incarnations.

This is the question, in fact, which most frequently appears in my mail. "Do you know anybody who can do what Edgar Cayce did?" people ask me. "I feel that if I knew about my past lives it would help me to understand what I am going through now."

Actually, I know of no clairvoyant who can match the variety, breadth, depth, scope, and overall validity of Edgar Cayce. I do know some clairvoyants whom I consider to be authentic—within limits—and honest (though not, I reiterate, infallible), whom I used to recommend when asked. But for reasons which have already been outlined in the previous chapter, I was always reluctant to do so, and whenever I did, it was always with the stated reservation that I could not guarantee performance.

I have known people to be greatly helped by a clairvoyant life reading. I have also known others who were not helped at all. Sometimes this failure was due to the fact that the reading was palpably inaccurate, as regards the character analysis at least. Sometimes it was due to the fact that the character analysis was all too accurate, and the person could not see, or refused to see, the truth about himself. So he labeled the reading "no good," in the manner of the monkey who called the mirror ugly.

There is, of course, another method of getting at one's own past-life history and that is through age-regression hypnosis. In this approach one relives (apparently) one or more past existences, often with considerable sensation, emotion, and stress. Age-regression has the merit of bringing, usually, a sense of inner conviction to those who experience it. It also often brings a certain kind of therapeutic catharsis; and so, whether the "past lives" are authentic memories or merely a fantasy creation of the mind, the experience has a pragmatic value at least.

But the method also has its dangers. In the hands of an unskilled operator much harm can be done. Hypnosis can be an open door to psychic experiences of many kinds, and in an emotionally unstable, insecure, or neurotic person the possibility of obsession or psychic invasion of one kind or another is always present. To enter into this sort of experiment for an evening's entertainment is, therefore, very unwise. It should be done seriously, in the proper surroundings, and with the motive of learning or of insight, not of amusement.

Still another method of tapping the past-life record is through the practice of meditation. The Rosicrucians suggest as a discipline the recalling of all the events of the day, in reverse order, every night before dropping off to sleep. Not only should the events be reviewed in the mind's eye, but their significance should be considered and one's own conduct evaluated in the light of one's own highest standards. It is stated that the faithful practice of this discipline will ultimately lead to the capacity to see one's past-life history, at first fragmentarily, and then with increasing clarity and detail.

Patanjali, in his classic handbook of yoga aphorisms,[1] includes the capacity to see past lives as one of the seventeen psychic powers attainable by one who practices yoga. According to the accounts of many travelers, this capacity is often achieved by Hindu yogis. They do not regard it as an important objective by itself, their purpose being to go beyond the knowledge of all transient things; but it is indicative at least of a considerable degree of spiritual progress.

Those people who object to reincarnation on the grounds that we do not remember our past are failing to take into account that the brain of the present body does not have recordings of the specific incidents of any other life experience but the present one. The memories of the past inhere in what might be called the "soul memory," or in that portion of the person called the Atman or the Over-Soul or the Sutratma—in other words, in that permanent Identity which periodically re-embodies for earth experience. Through meditation one stills the conscious mind processes and, once this habitual state of agitated thought is transcended, the center of consciousness of the personality-self becomes identified with the center of consciousness of the Soul-self. It is in this state that the memories of past lives are accessible and clear.

For various reasons meditation—accompanied by a life of altruism and service—may ultimately prove to be the

---

[1] *The Yoga Sutras of Patanjali.* These must be read with a commentary to be understood. Several excellent commentaries are available in English, including that of Swami Vivekananda in his book *Raja-Yoga* (Rama-krishna—Vivekananda Center, N.Y., 1955).

best path to self-knowledge and knowledge of one's past existences. Properly done, meditation carries with it the greatest spiritual and psychological safeguards. In this method the memories are not forced to the surface, nor is the knowledge of them likely to come prematurely. Their intimacy is preserved and their import is not likely to be misunderstood by an alien, though sympathetic, viewer. But it is a long road, and this is one of the reasons it is least traveled by. A man may spend a lifetime meditating and, though he garners many other spiritual and psychological benefits, he may never attain the vision of his past.

Moreover, even this ancient and honorable discipline is not beyond the fatuities of a certain type of mind. There are people who have only a superficial understanding of meditation as of many other things and who, while sitting and trying to hold their mind blank, see some visual images or receive some mental impressions which they then without more ado call a "past-life memory." I cannot help thinking of Little Jack Horner who sat in a corner, eating a Christmas pie; he put in his thumb and pulled out a plum, and said "Oh, what a good boy am I." For these meditating Jack Horners, or, more frequently, Jill Horners, are inclined to come up with past-life plums which they uncritically accept and complacently repeat to all and sundry. "I used to be a temple dancer in Egypt," they will say. "I got it in meditation." Or: "I played with Jesus as a child in Bethlehem. It came to me in meditation." To such an assertion there is nothing that one can say politely except that this is very interesting. But one would wish that all these earnest people would have a little more critical sense and a little less gullibility even with regard to themselves, and the phantasmagoria of their own minds.

I do not mean to disparage all such impressions. I am sure that many true things *are* obtained through meditation. But I personally would believe nothing that I or anybody else got "in meditation" unless I had means of substantiating it elsewhere. Obviously it would be difficult to prove that a person had or had not been a temple dancer in Egypt. But, assuming that this "came to her" in meditation, and assuming that all her life she had had a taste for exotic and rhythmic music, though all her family was quite unmusical; and assuming too that she has had a recurrent dream all her life in which, dressed as a dancer in a strangely lighted hall, she sees a sword descending over her head and then she awakes in terror; and assuming further that whenever she has visited a museum and gone through the Egyptian rooms she feels an odd sense of familiarity and apprehension; and assuming a number of other curious tastes, fears, impressions, incidents, and the like throughout her lifetime, then I would be willing to believe that possibly in meditation she *had* really tapped an authentic fragment of memory from the past. *Possibly.* But I would feel much more certain about it if a clairvoyant, or even two clairvoyants, independently and with no knowledge of any of these various subjective experiences, gave an account of such a past life which tallied point for point with the woman's impressions, and even enlarged upon them in a manner to account for things not previously understood by her. And I would feel still more confident about it if later, or better still, concurrently, she had been age-regressed by a competent hypnotherapist and relived the whole experience which point for point corresponded to what the clairvoyants said.

In this manner not only could a person's authentic past be reconstructed for his own psychological benefit, but also the case for reincarnation in general could be far more satisfactorily established than it ever has been up till now.

II

Curiosity about past lives, then, inevitably accompanies a new-found interest in reincarnation. But concerning the wisdom of such curiosity much can be said, pro and con.

In the lore of the Greeks, the gods traditionally dip all souls who are about to be born into the River of Forgetfulness; and, all things considered, this does seem a merciful provision. Someone has said that happiness consists in nothing more than a good digestion and a poor memory; and, in view of all the agonies of body and mind that most of us undergo in one lifetime, it really does seem the height of imprudence, if not of morbidity, to want to remember the pains, humiliations, and frustrations of a dozen more lifetimes.

One of the early Theosophical writers, W. Q. Judge, wrote uncompromisingly against such a quest. "The accounts of other incarnations," he wrote, "are neither useful nor reliable; they will do no good in the end but may lead to vanity or gloom, and therefore are to be avoided."

I would be willing to go along with Mr. Judge in part

at least. Many past-life accounts are *not* completely reliable. But I would challenge the statement that they are not useful, because, even when their reliability may have been only approximate, I have too frequently seen their very real usefulness. As to the proposition that they may lead to vanity or gloom, you might just as well say the same concerning a love affair; but this hardly seems sufficient reason for not taking a chance and enjoying it, for a time, come what may in the end. Besides, I would question the either-or nature of the proposition, contending that it may also lead to many other possible consequences in between vanity and gloom.

It must be remembered, of course, that Mr. Judge was writing in a pre-psychoanalytical period of history, and he cannot be expected therefore to have been aware of the values inherent in the guided exploration of the unconscious. It is a basic premise of psychoanalytical approaches that the discovery of the contents of the unconscious can lead to *insight,* and the insight can in turn make it possible to handle the problems of the present in a more mature and a more integrated way. Reincarnationist psychoanalysis would postulate the existence of a far deeper unconscious, stretching through centuries and centuries of time; and it would therefore make an effort to plumb these greater depths. The purpose would be similar, namely, the achievement of *insight.*

In recent years it has been increasingly recognized, of course, that insight is not always enough. It must be implemented, in more cases than not, by some daily discipline, some constructive program for living, before the individual can achieve mental and emotional health. And yet almost any practicing therapist would testify to the fact that there are cases in which the mere achievement of insight has had a transforming effect. From my own observation of reincarnationist cases I can assert positively that this can happen also on the basis of apparent past-life knowledge.

I think, for example, of the case of a frail but very pretty young woman whose every experience with men was an unhappy one. She married twice, and in both marriages she was neglected, humiliated, subjected to several varieties of mental cruelty, and finally abandoned. In a life reading she obtained she was told that in a former life she was in the male sex, and a lawyer by profession. The man had held the opinion common to his time and place, England of an earlier century, that women were men's mental inferiors. He married only for the sake of having a household convenience and treated his wife as a servant, never allowing her to share his social life or his intellectual interests, though the woman was capable of sharing them. The present-life situation, as a woman, then, was the karmic result of the former behavior as a man. Its educative purpose was to realize that women are not so inferior as some men would like to think, and that they can share and enrich a man's life if only he will let them. The coldness, neglect, and humiliation she met from the men of her present life were merely the reflection of her own previous conduct toward a woman.

There were no objective evidences that substantiated this past-life account, though there were several minor subjective evidences such as, for example, a strong disinclination for housework and cooking and a very rational clear-thinking mind, both of which traits could have been carry-overs from a recent male incarnation. At any event, whether true or not, this explanation gave the young woman a peace she had never known before, and for the first time in her adult life, an acceptance of her situation. The anxiety, stress, and resentment dissolved and she was able to meet life with new courage. She had been given a handle, so to speak, for what previously had been an impossibly unwieldy reality. I doubt if any other psychotherapeutic approach could have done the same in so short a space of time as the three quarters of an hour, or less, that it took for the life reading. I could cite many other similar examples.

On the other hand, it must also be recognized that the going back into past or presumable past lives can be carried to exaggerated lengths. If a tree is suffering from a storm-damaged branch one does not proceed to examine its roots. If a man's restaurant business if failing because he does not practice cleanliness there may be little utility in telling him that he used to be a prince in Atlantis; it would be more to the point to tell him to wash his silverware more carefully and keep his fingernails clean.

In short, above the surface there are immediate and contemporary causes for many of the difficulties we find ourselves in, and it is not only beside the point but a waste of time and even a way of evading the issue to go nosing about in ancient times.

Discrimination, then, is the key word. There are times to go back and there are times not to go back. And, whether one goes back or not, the fact remains that one must *change oneself* if any escape from a present painful situation is to be effected.

What I am saying here is no different, essentially, from what many psychotherapists have arrived at in recent years, in a strong reaction against the exaggerated claims of psychoanalysis. Andrew Salter is one who has not only dissented, but vehemently dissented, against the Freudian excesses. The outspoken opening sentence of one of his books[2] voices the sentiments—if a bit bluntly—of many another non-Freudian. "It is high time," he begins, "that psychoanalysis, like the elephant of the fable, dragged itself off into some distant jungle graveyard and died. . . ."

Salter was protesting not only against the "metaphysical quicksands" of Freud, and the "elaborately unscientific Freudian laws and regulations," but also against the long-drawn out, torturous, and often futile delvings into dreams and childhood memories. He proposed a method of re-training the human being for more effective handling of his problems on the basis of the well-established principle of the conditioned reflex. A dog can be taught to salivate at the ringing of a bell, if the bell has been rung every time he has been fed. He has a conditioned reflex. Human psychological problems are basically of this nature. The human being has been conditioned. He can be recondi-

2 *Conditioned Reflex Therapy* (The Creative Age Press, N.Y., 1949).

tioned, and thus "we can approach," Salter says, "human behavior in terms of fundamental components instead of metaphysical labels."

Other therapists who have taken a similar position with regard to the inutility of focusing on the past and the necessity of dealing directly with the present are Dr. Carl Rogers, with his nondirective therapy, and Dr. Abraham Low, with his Will Training therapy.

If men like Salter, Rogers, and Low ever came to accept the reincarnation theory, it could be expected that they would take a similar stand with regard to the knowledge of past lives. They might well acknowledge the reality of previous existences; but they would insist on the necessity of coming to grips with the present one, and retraining the self along the lines of healthy behavior *now*.

It is interesting to observe how the metaphysicians react to the matter of past lives. When I say "metaphysicians" I refer to those persons who follow some system of religiously oriented mental healing, generally known as "New Thought," which includes Unity, Religious Science, Divine Science, and various of their offshoots.

Some of the metaphysicians flatly deny the reality of reincarnation, and there is one "Truth teacher" in Los Angeles who goes so far as to say that the idea "simply nauseates" him.

It has been my observation of many of these metaphysicians that they often are not sufficiently well informed concerning the theory to know what they are being hostile to. Some of them take the position that life is a matter of "infinite progression" and that therefore it "cannot regress" to planet earth but goes ever onward and upward. It has always seemed to me that they have never given this question sufficiently careful thought, though the position they take sounds speciously reasonable. It is as if they announced to the principal of the grade school: "Education cannot regress. Therefore my child cannot return to the same school building every day! He must go ever upward and onward!"

One student of metaphysics with whom I discussed this point was quite disturbed at the thought of returning to this planet. "Why can't we go on learning on other planets?" she asked, almost belligerently. I do not doubt that we could; but the point is that if a lesson has to be mastered it will have to be mastered elsewhere as well as here, and so it might as well *be* here.

If a boy in the fifth grade moves with his family to another town in another state, he may joyfully anticipate a new freedom—just as metaphysicians seem joyfully to anticipate their vague but "infinite" progression. None the less, state laws will require that he continue going to school, and he will have to finish the fifth grade, or its educational equivalent, in whatever other school he attends. Possibly there are cosmic arrangements whereby souls *can* transfer from one planetary school to another; but our situation with regard to the lessons and grades of life can be no different from that of the schoolboy. In any case the whole question will finally have to be decided by evidence, not by wishful preference or even by reasoning; and whatever inferential evidences we already have point to the fact that a good many souls *do* return right here.

There are other metaphysicians, however, who *are* well informed concerning reincarnation, and who privately accept it. But publicly they deny their belief, or disguise it; or they evade the subject as long as possible. Perhaps this is because they feel that the concept of karma will have a discouraging or negative effect on people who want to make "demonstrations" of health, happiness, prosperity, and a true mate. They may be right. But I cannot be in sympathy with an outlook that insists, publicly or privately, that it is everybody's "divine right" as "a child of God" to have health, happiness, prosperity, and a true mate when he has certain outstanding debts to pay the universe because of the misuse of such gifts before; when he has not yet outgrown serious immaturities of character; and when he still has a hard core of egotism which makes him undeserving of these blessings, or incapable of keeping them for long even if by some metaphysical *tour de force* he managed to get them.

A materialistic and ego-centered emphasis on what they want and what they feel they deserve is in fact the point at which many metaphysicians not only reason sophistically, but also part company with the true aims of genuine religion. Metaphysicians usually call their system "religious," either implicitly or explicitly (as "Divine Science" or "Religious Science"), and they usually teach their ideas in the churches which they establish. But if they claim to be religious, they should understand that the perfection of spiritual being, not the gratification of self-will and personality desires, should be their primary emphasis.

This is not to say that I disparage metaphysics or the practice of its disciplines. On the contrary, I think that many of their techniques are both psychologically sound and efficacious. I also think it is possible for people to begin the cancellation, as it were, of their karma, or the more rapid repayment of it, through the sustained efforts at changing their consciousness with the methods which metaphysical teachers have so ably set forth. "Be ye transformed," Jesus said, "by the renewing of your mind." How else, indeed, can karma be ultimately transcended but by the changing of the thinking patterns? And an explicit daily discipline such as the metaphysicians insist on is one of the best ways I know for the changing of habitual ways of thought. So I am basically in sympathy with some of their approaches. I take exception to them only when they seem to take an irresponsible attitude toward their past or present obligations, or a too crassly materialistic or hedonistic attitude toward the goods of this world.

There are a good many metaphysicians, however, who fully acknowledge the truth of reincarnation, both privately and publicly, and who find in it no threat to the efficacy of their own approach, as indeed there should not be if both are realistically understood. A man's present situation in life represents the sum total of what he has thought— and therefore done—in the past. And his future situation in life will similarly represent all that he is thinking—and doing—now. The full truth of this is not always appreciable in one life span, since some causes mature only with a long passage of time; and many seeming discrepancies exist in people's lives which would seem to invalidate the equivalence of thinking and destiny. So actually the metaphysicians' basic contention as to the causative power of thought is strengthened rather than weakened by the many-life theory.

Moreover, if a metaphysician had some inkling as to the past-life causation of a present-life difficulty, he could devise thought methods, whether "affirmations," "treatments," or "daily meditations" which would with greater precision get at the roots of a problem, rather than at superficial and maybe irrelevant aspects of it.

There is still another group of metaphysicians whose stand in the matter resembles, in a way, the psychotherapists who do not wish to go into depth causation but prefer to focus on the present moment. These metaphysicians say, essentially: Reincarnation may be true. In fact it probably is. But it is of no real importance to know about past lives because the important thing is the transformation of the self *now*. If one looks backward, like Lot's wife, one can crystallize. One must look upward, in the direction of God. One must look inward, to the luminous essence within. One must act in this awareness, and from this inner center. A gratified curiosity about past lives with their errors and confusions is of no use for this act of surrender. A spiritual about-face is what is important.

I must say that I am completely in agreement with this point of view. But not all people are capable of an approach or a surrender of this kind.

All things considered, I have come to the following conclusions on the question of knowing about past lives.

First, I believe it is of importance, in the present stage of
human history, that research into past-life histories be done
for the sake of establishing a true science of depth psychology. Only in this way can psychotherapy and religion be
given scientific foundations as regards human behavior and
its alterations. Only in this way can human destiny be understood.

Second, I believe that it can be of great value to some
people to make the effort to learn something about their
own past lives. In this manner they can acquire insight into
their own contradictions, frustrations, inadequacies, and
fixations. Insight is not of itself miraculous, either in
Freudian or reincarnationist psychoanalysis; but reincarnationist insight is more efficacious, I believe, than any
other kind, because it takes place in the framework of a
philosophy of cosmic purposiveness rather than of cosmic
meaninglessness. It can, therefore, liberate energy and lead
to self-transformation in a manner that insight obtained in
the gloomy, materialistic, spirit-negating, and atheistic
Freudian system cannot.

Third, I believe that some people should not waste time
with the attempt to discover their own past lives, primarily
because they really do not need to know them. Their problems exist more in relation to present-life causation than to
past. There is another and smaller group of people who
should not waste time with past lives because they have
reached that point of evolution where they are capable of

spiritual discipline and a sustained quest for God-awareness, and the knowledge of past lives becomes irrelevant and unnecessary. But I would venture to guess that this second group of people constitutes only about one per cent of the total population.

Fourth, I believe that there are many people who might benefit greatly from the knowledge of their own past lives but who are unable to discover what they were. They are not good hypnotic subjects; they know of no good clairvoyant; they are not capable of the disciplines of meditation. But they need not feel unduly thwarted. Millions of people have lived out their lives and fulfilled their life purpose without such knowledge; millions more can, and will, do so. Any human being who lives by the simple but profound rule of doing unto others—plant, animal, and human—as he would be done by; who earnestly seeks to fulfill his life duties; who tries to be of service to his fellow creatures; and who seeks to govern the cravings of the body self is doing what he is supposed to be doing anyway, whether he knows his past lives or not.

I recall a homely philosophic riddle that goes: Why does a man have two ears and one mouth? to which the answer was: So that he can listen twice as much as he talks. And I seem also dimly to remember another, which goes: Why does a man have eyes in the front of his head? to which the answer seems to have been: So that he can look where he is going, not where he is coming from.

A man can turn his head backward, it is true. And sometimes he must, to get his bearings. But *most of the time,* he must look, and walk, forward. This is simply the wisdom of common sense. Reincarnation may be an uncommon doc-trine, in our part of the world; but that is all the more rea-son why it should be approached with eminent common sense.

As for myself, in case anyone is curious about it, I do not know with certainty any of my own past lives. Various clair-voyants have told me of this or that previous incarnation. Sometimes what they said had an authentic ring, and some-times not. In no case have I had sufficient corroborating evi-dence to feel that I really know the truth of the matter. There is one thing that I do know, however, with dreadful and depressing certainty, and that is my many deficiencies of character. From these I can infer certain experiences in the past, possibly even in certain countries because of a strong feeling I have for them, but these are inferences, and nothing more.

Even if I knew my past incarnations with precision, how-ever, I doubt that I would discuss them in public. And, once I had extracted from them the clues to what I should be doing with my present lifetime, I doubt that I would dwell upon them very much or very often. There are those who might not agree with me on this, but I am inclined to think in this connection of what a diplomat once said when he was asked whether or not it was necessary in the field of diplomacy to know Latin. "No," he said, after a moment's consideration, "it is sufficient to have forgotten it."

This has always seemed to me both a wise and a witty re-mark, and I was quite surprised one time, in quoting it to a friend, to hear him say he did not understand it. I explained, as best I could, that the study of Latin gives one a sense of familiarity with the root words and the grammatical structure of English as well as of several other modern European languages. Hence, even a hazy recollection of one's high-school Latin can be very valuable; in fact, having a hazy recollection of it may even be better than having a present total recall to clutter up one's mind.

It has often occurred to me that one might well paraphrase the diplomat's remark and apply it to reincarnation. Is it necessary to know one's past lives? . . . No. . . . It is sufficient to have forgotten them. . . . And lest someone be puzzled by what I mean, let me explain: A knowledge of reincarnation as the basic structure of life places one's present lifetime in both a healthy and an intelligible perspective; and an acquaintance with some of one's own positive and negative karma from the past can give one a sense of the roots from which one's present virtues and one's present problems spring. But it is almost better (in our present stage of evolution) to have all this in the background of one's mind than to have it as an ever-present and paramount preoccupation.

There is a hymn, attributed to the Sanskrit, which is, I think, apropos to the whole question.

THE SALUTATION OF THE DAWN

Listen to the exhortation of the dawn!
Look to this day, for it is life,
The very life of life!
In its brief course lie all the verities
And all the realities of your existence:
The bliss of growth; the glory of action;

The splendour of beauty.
For yesterday is but a dream,
And tomorrow is only a vision.
But today well-lived makes every yesterday a dream of
*   happiness,*
And every tomorrow a vision of hope.
Look well, therefore, to this day.
Such is the salutation of the dawn.

5

MANY LIVES, MANY LOVES
Reincarnation and Love

At first glance it may seem a bit incongruous to associate so dramatic a subject as love with so theoretical a subject as reincarnation; but in actuality there may be a very vital and very important connection between the two.

This connection first became apparent to me when I was studying the clairvoyant records of Edgar Cayce. As many people know, Cayce gave a strange kind of study, called a life reading, on many hundreds of people. These readings constituted a kind of psychoanalysis of the persons in question, with these significant differences from the usual psychoanalysis: 1) they were given while Cayce was lying on a couch rather than the person being analyzed; 2) they were frequently given with distances of many miles between Cayce and the person being analyzed, on the basis merely of a name, address, and birth date; and 3) they accounted for the present-life situation in terms of some past-life causation.

While these readings have their own limitations, they certainly do add important evidence for the validity of clairvoyance as a faculty of the human mind; and while they cannot fairly be said to constitute proof of reincarnation, they at least provide a kind of circumstantial evidence.

Certainly the case histories of all these hundreds of people do give the theory of reincarnation a new immediacy. Coming upon them with a background in Theosophical thought and some knowledge of Hinduism and Buddhism, I myself felt as if, to the skeleton of a hypothesis, I suddenly saw the addition of flesh, muscle, nerve currents, and the throbbing pulsation of life.

I set myself the task, then, of setting forth as best I could the evidence for reincarnation that seemed to be contained within those readings, of systematizing the case history material, and of formulating some tentative principles of karmic law. I tried also to integrate these conclusions with the data of modern psychology, and at the same time to show the essential agreement of the reincarnation principles with the basic teachings of Christ. *Many Mansions,* published in 1950, is the result of that effort.

It seemed to me at the time that the dramatic and often tragic material in those files constituted a kind of symphony of human suffering. "Men are born; they suffer; they die" seemed to sound a fateful motif comparable to the trumpet notes sounded at the very beginning of Tchaikovsky's Fourth Symphony; and the whole book became in my conception of it a kind of composition on suffering, Theme and Variations. Almost every chapter, therefore, was intended to present a new facet of human pain, though I tried to state it in a major key of hope and optimism rather than in a minor one of melancholy, because pain, I was convinced, is meaningful and life is full of purpose.

I do not think that, were I to do it again, I would now revise my original conception. Suffering *is* basic to, and implicit in, the human situation; how much more so, in that long process of human evolvement which we call reincarnation. But in the years since then I have from time to time seen how other secondary emphases could be made on the basis of the same material. For a time it seemed to me that balance was an important philosophical and practical emphasis; the book *The World Within* was the result.

I do not now feel impelled to write a new book establishing another emphasis of this material; I feel that I have said almost all that I wish to say about the Cayce data. But in recent months I have been giving a good deal of thought to the subject of love; and it has seemed to me that, in a very special way, the subject is illumined and thrown into clearer perspective by the reincarnation theory.

For pain is, as Gibran put it, the breaking of the shell that encloses our understanding. It is the bitter potion by which the physician within us heals our sick self. Our sick self is a selfish self, and a disproportionate one. The physician within has as one aim the beautiful achievement of balance, and as another, the beautiful achievement of love.

Love being a matter of the relationship of one unit of life to another, it is worth noting that in the Cayce data there is a basic proposition regarding human relationships. It can be stated as follows:

Souls who were closely related in one lifetime tend to meet in other lifetimes. If the relationship was one of love,

*the love persists; if one of enmity, the enmity must be over-
come; if one of obligation, the obligation must be paid.*

This is a plausible proposition, surely; for if we grant the
continuity of life at all, and the operation of law governing
it, it would seem likely that the powerful force of attraction
between souls would have its own strong persistence; and
wherever there has been hatred, deeds surely must have
been done which require karmic rectification and hence a
renewed association. Even in a love relationship there is
usually a mixture of good and of bad; and all of us must
have incurred debts therefore which we must pay, or de-
served rewards which must be delivered.

For the full understanding of human relationships several other propositions must be taken into consideration.

*Souls incarnate sometimes as a man and sometimes as a
woman.*

This idea is sometimes repugnant to people—men and
women alike—but, apart from the evidence that exists for
it, the alternation of sex is both psychologically and philosophically reasonable. For how else could the soul achieve
a well-rounded balance unless it had been both active and
passive, both dominant and subservient, both positive and
negative, in many experiences?

*Evolving souls incarnate sometimes in one race and
sometimes in another.*

This notion, too, is abhorrent to some people—principally to those who consciously or unconsciously are convinced of the superiority of their own present race. There
is considerable evidence to substantiate race change as well
as sex change; and it is not only philosophically and psy-

chologically but also anthropologically reasonable that such changes must take place. The history of mankind has been long and varied, and the races that now exist in certain relations of dominance and subservience are different from races that existed before in other patterns of relationship.

There are other important basic concepts, of course, but these three are of particular significance as regards human relationships. If we grant the truth of these propositions, we will see at once that a fascinating series of permutations and combinations must take place. In one existence two entities may know each other as friend and friend; in the next as parent and child; in another as sister and brother; in still another as husband and wife. In one incarnation entity A may be a male in Turkey, who abuses and mistreats entity B, a female slave in his harem. In the following incarnation entity B may be a male in Japan, and entity A, his wife, is completely under his domination. In one life experience an entity may be an Indian, made a slave by invading Spaniards and brutally mistreated; in the following life experience the same entity may be a white man, determined to see that justice be done to the defrauded American Indians, for whom he feels a peculiar sympathy.

These basic considerations suggest an analogy. Any human life situation is like the momentary position of a kaleidoscope; and the group of souls within that situation are like the bits of brightly colored glass which form an interesting pattern of relationship. Then the kaleidoscope is shaken by the Lords of Life, so to speak, and with this flick of the wrist there comes into being a new design, a new combination of elements. And so on, again and again, time after time, always different, always beautiful.

The image is incomplete, of course. Perhaps it is misleading. I do not mean to imply that there is a fixed number of souls, constantly being reshuffled. New elements and new individuals must always be entering the situation. All that I mean to say is that we do come together, again and again; and sometimes, if I may strain the kaleidoscope analogy, the juxtaposition of pieces is a jagged and uncomfortable one. But always it is significant, and always there is a dynamic and purposeful intention, even though this may not always be superficially apparent to the participators. The soul-self remembers, even though the personality-self does not.

An interesting illustration of this submerged awareness can be seen in a rather strange story told me recently by a highly respected Episcopalian priest. In his youth he had been a test pilot and later a musician in a symphony orchestra. One night he had the startling experience of finding himself outside of his own body, looking down on it as it lay on the bed. He was then aware of being given instruction by some presence in another "dimension." After some time he found himself back again in his body, but the experience was repeated again and again. As a result of this training he became clairvoyant, clairaudient, and aware of many of his own past lives. He also became intensely desirous of helping other people in some kind of spiritual relationship. Though a mature adult and one never before interested in religion, he left his career as a musician to study in a theological seminary. He related to me a vividly recalled past-life experience when, as a priest in Atlantis, he liberated a group of persons from a dungeon. The other priests discovered what he had done and as punishment strapped him to a chair and with a large mallet bludgeoned him to death. The persons whom he had freed learned of what had happened, but were powerless to help him. In the present lifetime he knew a family every member of which seemed unusually desirous of helping him in every way possible. Curious as to the reason for this almost excessive kindness, which to him seemed undeserved, he looked upon them clairvoyantly and saw that the group of people whom he had freed from a terrible fate in Atlantis had come together in this closely knit family now; and that in every one of them there lay deep within a sense of gratitude and obligation. . . .

A story of this type is beyond verification, of course, in any strict objective sense. It would not meet any of the criteria set up by Dr. Stevenson for cases of past-life recall. So we can evaluate it only on the basis of the integrity, intelligence, and general rationality of the man telling it, and at best accept it in a tentative way. But in any case the principles involved are precisely what we find in the Cayce readings, with which the priest was unfamiliar; namely, that souls closely knit in any relationship in one lifetime tend to come together in other lifetimes, and there are bonds of obligation between them.

Sometimes this obligation is felt and voluntarily discharged, as in the aforementioned case. Other times the obligation is felt, but the payment is so difficult that it is enforced by the inextricability of circumstances. Whenever we see an unbearably difficult life situation, from which there seems to be no escape, we can rest assured that the participants in it are held there by the long arm of karmic law—which means, really, by the consequence of some previous conspicuous failure to love.

A wife, for example, who has a neurotically critical and abusive husband with whom she is extremely unhappy, yet cannot leave because of four small children, can be almost certain that she is in this situation because she has some obligation to this soul who is her husband as well as to these souls who are her children. Another case would be that of a young man, the sole support of an aged and sickly mother, who would like to marry but because of lack of education and training is unable to support both a wife and a mother. He loves his mother and does not wish to abandon her to charity; and so he is faced with the prospect of long years of bachelorhood and sacrifice. It is admittedly a painful situation. But perhaps in another lifetime and in other circumstances he had neglected the welfare of this being who is now his mother, and now he is given the opportunity of rectifying the neglect.

"Love is the fulfilling of the law," Jesus said, and we may well interpret this to mean that as soon as a person can truly learn to love the disagreeable or restrictive person with whom he is involved, he will be released from the bondage.

This, then, is the first effect of the long-range point of view on life; it gives insight into relationships that seem unbearably difficult.

Another effect is to clarify what seem to be irrational

attractions between people, especially relationships which seem strange, bizarre, or somehow indefensible by conventional standards.

Homosexuality, for example, is a love expression which rouses much antagonism among heterosexual people. Often we see two homosexual men (or women) establishing a home together and living together as man and wife. However well-ordered their domestic arrangement, and however constructive their contribution to society otherwise, most people tend to despise such a relationship and look upon it with reactions ranging from contemptuous disgust to sophisticated amusement. I personally do not feel that homosexuality is the best solution of man's sexual predicament; the whole universe seems to be founded on the principle of polarity and therefore the normal male-female attachment seems to be more in alignment with cosmic principles.

However, on the path of growth, aberrations and irregularities *do* appear. A being who has been in the female body many times and then incarnates in a male body may find it extremely difficult to act in an acceptable masculine manner; so called "effeminacy" is then conspicuous, making it both psychologically and biologically difficult for the person to play the male role. The individual may not masculinize himself, so to speak, in this lifetime; but he will at least have been made aware of his weaknesses and hence better prepared to complete the balancing process in the succeeding life.

An interracial marriage is another relationship of which people generally tend to disapprove. The soldier who marries a Japanese girl, the white woman who marries a black man, the American woman who marries a Filipino—the mere mention of such alliances may cause some persons to feel an immediate sense of antagonism. This is perhaps a throwback to the early history of the human race when a marriage outside the tribal group was considered dangerous and tabu; perhaps it is due to that egocentricity which characterizes all races and causes them to believe their own racial group is superior.

But whatever the origin of the antagonism, the whole situation falls into an entirely different perspective when viewed from a reincarnationist point of view.

Could it be possible that the American soldier and the Japanese girl were man and wife before, both of them Japanese in that lifetime, or both of them Americans? Could it not be conceivable that the white girl who married the black man was a slaveowner in early America who incurred a serious debt to the soul of the black slave who, again as a black, is now her husband? Could it not have happened that the American girl and the Filipino boy were brothers centuries ago in Crete, and one betrayed the other for reasons of social advantage, so that now this soul is given the opportunity of redeeming the betrayal by a loyalty even in the face of social ostracism?

Similar considerations can be brought to bear on any other type of unusual love relationship, whether the disparity between the partners be one of social standing, wealth, education, age, or intelligence.

I do not mean to imply that all foolish relationships and all trivial affairs in the present are to be excused in the

name of a past-life involvement, or that karma should become the alibi for every present-life folly. All too many
people confuse bad management with destiny, and bad
judgment in the present with karmic necessity from the
past. I am merely saying that in some instances, perhaps
most instances, of a strong intense relationship between
people—especially when that relationship is difficult and
inescapable, or when it is not conventional, usual, or ex-
plicable in ordinary terms—the roots of the relationship
are to be looked for in the past.

The result of this point of view is to promote a less critical and more tolerant attitude on the part of the observer.
This of itself is no small matter. A newspaper in Ontario
once carried this announcement: "You may notice some
typographical errors in this paper. They were put in inten-
tionally. This paper tries to print something for everybody
and some people are not happy unless they find mistakes."
And this sums up a typical human propensity.

Across the street from the public library in downtown
Los Angeles there stands, visible for many blocks around, a
high, huge, neon-lit sign reading: JESUS SAVES. It is a sign
which must have meaning for a great many people; at least
it has stood there for many years at the annual cost of
heaven knows what on the part of the Bible School which
supports it. But every time I see it it sets me wondering
what words I would erect in neon lights, given the permission and the wherewithal to do so.

The sentence that I usually decide upon is: JUDGE NOT
THAT YE BE NOT JUDGED—largely because I find truth in it
at so many levels of truth and because a day hardly passes

that I do not observe how quick people are to judge and criticize. Criticism is an unfortunate, even a dangerous, habit. Dangerous, I say, because if the Cayce readings are to be believed, serious karmic consequences can be set in motion by critical speech. The circumstances which we pass judgment on become our own situation at some future time, so that we can come to understand the inner necessity for everything.

The realization that each man's life, and each woman's life, with all its peculiarities and aberrations and its love relationships or the lack of them, is precisely the best situation in which this soul can work out its own life sums can give our critical tongues pause. "My life is not a spectacle but a *life,*" Emerson said. It is a wise thought, and one worth remembering both with regard to oneself and with regard to others.

The many-life hypothesis, then, clarifies much in human relationships, and through the clarification helps us to become less intolerant. It also leads to a sense of spiritual perspective and an understanding of the purpose behind all love experiences.

I remember when I was going to college I saw a little item in the college paper which went like this:

> Boy: Do you love me?
> Girl: I love everybody.
> Boy: Leave that to God. We should specialize.

When other items of far greater importance in my college curriculum have long since escaped me, I cannot imagine why this one should have made such a lasting impression; but the fact remains that it did.

The boy was right, of course; we must specialize. The conditions of the drama in which we are all acting require that we narrow our attention down to one person, at least for a period of time. In our Judeo-Christian culture people are theoretically expected to pick out one mate and live with him or her for so long as they both shall live, though in practice, as we all know, it often amounts to no more than for as long as they both can stand it. In any case this narrowing of attention and scope has many good effects, however painful it may sometimes be. It keeps people to task, and it is educative in many subtle and obvious ways.

But the girl was right, too. She "loved everybody," she said, though in all probability she only *thought* she loved everybody. . . . "Loving everybody" is an illusion common among idealists, churchgoers, and metaphysicians, and one that is quickly shattered when put to any truly rigorous test. But none the less we must all ultimately come to the point of really loving all living creatures, and it would seem that the many vicissitudes of love have this end in view.

To lose a beloved person by death, for example, is a very painful experience. Ferenc Molnar, the Hungarian playwright, wrote feelingly on this subject. He related an old Greek legend about a couple who loved each other dearly. One day they did a favor to a god who was traveling in disguise. The god, later making his identity known, offered to grant any desire they wished. The two looked at each other, and of one accord spoke, saying that they desired the great boon of dying at exactly the same moment, so that neither would know the pain of separation. This was Molnar's favorite story, he said, and anyone who has experienced the grief of loss can well appreciate its pathos.

In Buddhist lore there is the equally touching story of the woman who had lost her husband and not long after her only son by death. Half crazed with grief she sought out the Buddha asking him to restore her son to life. The Compassionate One looked at her with deep pity in his eyes and said, gently, "If you will bring me a grain of wheat from a household where there has been no death, I will restore your son to you." Eagerly the woman began her search from door to door and from village to village. But in every household where she made her query she learned that here, too, there had been death. Finally the woman understood the lesson that Buddha was trying to teach her. She knew now that death was a universal experience and sooner or later loss comes to us all. She knew too that she must put aside her grieving and begin to live her life anew.

There are many lessons to be learned from loss, but perhaps one of the most important ones is this: that there is something lovable in all creatures, and the love that has been concentrated in one person can be distributed to many. This is, like most things, far more easily said than done, especially when one has been for years the recipient of a warm affection and when there has been a companionship that cannot be easily replaced. But perhaps one must learn to be a more active giver of love, especially to those who are needy of it whether these be neighbors and friends or whether they be strangers whom one makes the effort now to find.

Another one of the painful vicissitudes of love is to lose the beloved to another human being. Can a man love two girls at the same time? someone asked an Advice to the Lovelorn columnist. Yes, came the answer, until one of the girls finds out. . . . The moment of finding out can be a very terrible one, especially to a marriage partner, whether woman or man, in a relationship of long standing. The experience can in fact be far more devastating to some people than loss by death; for while death is irrevocable, at least one can usually cherish the memory (or the illusion!) of an inviolate love; whereas with love lost to another person, one feels a sense of betrayal and rejection which is very difficult to bear.

This is true even if one feels that the new love is destined to an early conclusion. There is comfort to be found perhaps in the Japanese fable of the two teardrops who met on the stream of time. "Where do you come from?" asked one teardrop of the other. "I am the tear of a woman who lost her beloved to another woman," was the answer. "She should not have grieved so," replied the other. "I am the tear of the woman to whom she lost him." But, while the ironic truth of this fable applies in many and many an instance, it does not apply in all; to say nothing of the fact that the most enduring kind of fortitude cannot arise, or subsist, merely upon the disaster of a rival.

Whatever the ultimate outcome, a triangle is almost inevitably a shattering experience, and it is certainly a very common one. From the point of view of reincarnation, some light can be brought to bear upon the problem if we recall that in our many past existences we have had close bonds of affection with many people. Should one of these people, at a certain juncture of our life, chance to come again within our sphere, the ancient attraction is likely to flare again; and all considerations of loyalty or propriety can swiftly take flight. This is not to be considered as an excuse for infidelity; it is only to be considered as a partial explanation of the causes of it.

But once again, whatever the underlying reason, and whatever its point of origin in the past or in the present, the fact remains that this vicissitude, too, is educative. For the two who are entering the new and sometimes illicit relationship it imparts on the one hand a new excitement and a new luster to life. It is on the other hand a test of conscience, character, and all the basic values by which they live. For the third person, the excluded one, it is a severer test of every resource of endurance, philosophy, and character than for the other two. Frequently the experience can result in new and sometimes shocking self-knowledge. Often the emptiness in the life can lead to the cultivation of new talents and new interests, and to ventures which would never have been attempted otherwise. So, from the long perspective, the devastation of being the odd angle of a triangle can be seen as a marvelous prelude to expansions of consciousness. Ultimately, of course, the experience can serve to teach the great, the difficult, and the subtle lesson of detachment. It is not a kindergarten lesson, this, but one that only near-graduates can learn: the lesson of releasing a beautiful thing, and relinquishing it willingly either to life itself or to the enjoyment of another.

There is another very widespread vicissitude of love, and that is the loss of it not by death or to another person, but by disillusionment.

A woman once testified in an annulment hearing in St. Louis that her husband had misrepresented himself to her before marriage, and that he had married her only for her money. In taking the case under advisement, the judge commented that if he were to grant annullments in all cases where there was misrepresentation, he would be doing nothing else—that all marriages were based on some kind of misrepresentation. . . . He had, I believe, a valid point.

In each of us is the understandable wish to appear well in the eyes of others. The masquerades we indulge in may range all the way from the most flagrant kinds of self-disguise down to the most innocent kinds of camouflage. But in addition to the weaknesses and defects of which we are secretly aware, and which we hope others will not notice, there are all those hidden weaknesses of which we ourselves are unaware and which only the tests and the emergencies of life bring to the surface. Many a woman thinks of herself as sweet, loving, and patient in the early years of marriage; but a husband's unfounded jealousy or a child's annoying behavior may cause her little by little to manifest qualities that are anything but sweet, loving, and patient.

Emerson has some interesting things to say apropos of this matter in his essay on Love. He is discussing the destiny of lovers. "But the lot of humanity," he says, "is on these children. Danger, sorrow, and pain arrive to them as to all. . . . The soul which is in the soul of each, craving for a perfect beatitude, detects incongruities, defects, and disproportion in the behavior of the other. Hence arise surprise, expostulation, and pain. . . . Their once flaming regard is sobered by time in either breast, and losing in violence what it gains in extent, it becomes a thorough good understanding. . . . Thus we are put in training for a love which knows not sex, or person, or partiality, but which seeks virtue and wisdom everywhere. . . ."

Emerson's thought here brings to mind a very striking passage in one of Plato's dialogues. We pass from the love of one beautiful object to another, Plato says, until finally we are capable of loving the beauty that is shining through all objects and persons, and of loving that supreme beauty which is God Himself.

Any person who can even tentatively accept the theory of reincarnation, and who feels that it is incumbent upon him to work diligently upon his own evolution, can find both solace and inspiration in this idea. If one of the purposes of our evolution is, as Plato suggests, as do also Christ and Buddha and all great religious teachers, that our love must become all-embracing, then the immediate sorrows of a particular love are less crushing to the spirit. The purpose of any loss of love is that we shall know expansion. A broken heart leads to a vessel of greater capacity.

You have lost your beloved by death, or to another person? Then let your love flow to other persons in a similarly painful situation, all over the world, and let it take practical, serviceable form. You have lost a much cherished child? Then remember that every living creature is the child of someone. Choose whichever category most appeals to your sympathies—crippled children; children orphaned by war; the grown-up children of Skid Row; the displaced children of revolution; or the little creatures in the city Animal Shelter, children of some mother cat or dog, helpless and lonely and terrified in the human jungle we have made. Let your love extend to them. You have been disillusioned in your love? Then remember Emerson's telling phrase: you have thus been put in training for a love which knows not sex, or person, or partiality, but which seeks virtue and wisdom everywhere.

It is an odd thing that the educational systems of all civilized countries should pay so much attention to the development of intelligence and no attention at all to the development of love. Perhaps it is because love has for so long been disparagingly regarded as a passion and as an emotion; and intelligence has long been considered to be the obvious superior of these. But what we have failed to take into account is that intelligence, too, has its two lower levels: the cunning of self-preservation and the shrewdness of self-advancement. Only at its highest level does it become intellect, the capacity to solve objective problems of science or of society.

We must come to realize that love the passion and love the emotion likewise have their higher level: love the quality; and it is this which we must all seek to cultivate.

Krishnamurti was once asked to sum up his teachings. He did so in six simple words: *Learn to think and to love.*

And it is this commandment that to me seems almost the epitome of the practical reincarnationist philosophy.

Both the quality of love and the capacity of intellect need to be consciously developed. We have, I believe, many lifetimes in which to develop them. Little by little, through our sorrows, our losses, and our many mistakes, both our insight and our sympathies enlarge. From the personal to the universal, from the selfish to the unselfish, from the passion to the quality, in ever-expanding concentric circles our love nature expands, concurrently as the light of our understanding increases. Finally there is that perfect balance of love and of intellect which is called wisdom.

And this is the purpose, I believe, of our many lives and our many loves.

6

Reincarnation and Literature

I

A rather droll commentary on the temperament of the German people has been attributed to the psychologist Jung. "If, when we die," he said, "we see before us two signposts, one reading: *To Heaven* and the other: *To Lectures about Heaven,* all the Germans will go to the lectures. . . ." The saying has also been applied to Unitarians, I am told, and very possibly to other cerebral types; but regardless of who actually said it first, and about whom, the saying certainly applies to a great many of us who find academic pursuits fascinating, often at the expense of practical ones.

This being such a practical time in human history, and such a scientific one, and one of such desperate urgency, I feel a little self-conscious, I must admit, about taking up anybody's time with a discussion of reincarnation as a theme of literature. On the face of it, this might appear as a very dull and academic concern—about on a par with Ph.D. theses on The Use of the Semicolon in the Comedies of Shakespeare or A Critical Analysis of Transitive and Intransitive Verbs in Six Presidential Addresses.

But actually a tracing of the reincarnation theme in literature is not quite so pedantic and stuffy a matter as it might ostensibly seem. It has, in fact, some very practical values and at times some very entertaining ones. To be sure, the fact that at least several hundred major and minor Western writers of prose and poetry have written about reincarnation proves absolutely nothing as to the truth of the theory. But—since writers tend to be in the upper rather than the lower ranges of intelligence—it does clearly indicate that an interest in the subject is perfectly compatible with genuine intellectual competence.

For one thing, then, an acquaintance with the many literary treatments of reincarnation becomes reassuring, in a way, to those of us who accept the idea. We are so widely regarded as muddle-headed dupes by most intellectuals of our times that it is nice to know that we are on this point at least in the same league with William Butler Yeats, Robert Browning, and the Poet Laureate of England.

For another thing, it is convenient for those of us who have something of the missionary spirit on this subject to have a few choice names up our sleeves, so to speak, to slip into the conversation when talking with the uninformed. It is worth a good deal, for example, in terms of missionary satisfaction, to say to a friend who is mad for Walt Whitman: "Oh, yes. Whitman. He believed in reincarnation, you know." This remark may be met with a look of polite surprise, indignant disbelief, or feigned stolidity; but in any case a seed has been sown, and it may come to good fruition.

After we have substantiated our point with some well-chosen and unmistakable quotations from *Leaves of Grass* we hope, of course, that our friend will look with awakened respect and fresh perspective on the reincarnation idea, since he now knows that his idol believed in it also. But we must be realistic enough to know that this may not happen at all. He may simply shut his mind to the whole matter, fencing off Whitman's belief in reincarnation as a whim, a poetic fancy, or one of those lapses of sanity so frequent among poets. Or, what is worse, he may begin to feel a certain disillusionment with Whitman, and begin to reappraise his grand passion. If Whitman could be so feebleminded as to believe in all that Oriental nonsense, maybe Whitman is not so great a poet as once he thought. And so he changes allegiances, and we have accomplished nothing but the alienation of somebody's literary affections. We cannot be sued for it, of course, but it does seem such a pity.

The risk may prove to be worth taking, however. For if our friend is intelligent, and if we later point out to him that his new poetic passion—say Kahlil Gibran, for example—also believed in reincarnation; and if we then acquaint him with the curious facts that the electric light he reads by was invented by a man who believed in reincarnation; and the Ford he drives to the public library was invented by a man who believed in reincarnation; and the American public library system itself was founded in 1731 by Benjamin Franklin, who also believed in reincarnation —the accumulation of small shocks may finally begin to take effect, and we will have succeeded in bringing one more person to a sensible view of the universe.

But there is still another very practical value in knowing about the literary treatments of reincarnation, and that is the practical value to be found in all good literature. A thoughtful writer's treatment of the basic issues of human life helps us to understand them better and to relate more adequately to our own life situation and to the other human beings who share it. Writers have always taken the great new philosophic and scientific concepts of their times and humanized them, so to speak; clothed them in flesh and blood; made them available to the common man in terms he can understand.

Writers about reincarnation have done this also. To be sure, a few of them have themselves misunderstood—in my opinion—the idea. Some of them have made fictional use, for example, of the idea of Eternal Recurrence as proposed by Nietzsche, Ouspensky, and others, namely, the mathematical notion that everything in the universe keeps repeating itself, down to the minutest detail, at recurring future points in time, and that a sense of premonition is the memory of events experienced in previous cycles.

J. B. Priestley took this concept as the basis of his play *I Have Been Here Before* and carried it off successfully, to judge by the critical acclaim of the time. However, he was dramatizing what in my estimation is an exceedingly unfortunate misconception. There is truth, of course, in the cyclic recurrence notion; but it can be both subtly and grossly misunderstood. Reincarnation makes psychological sense only if it is seen as an evolutionary and in a sense spiral process. The eternal recurrence idea, if it is regarded as a mechanical and absolutely repetitive process, is in my opinion both nightmarish and unbelievable, and can alienate those who might otherwise find the theory of the soul's return a plausible and helpful one. But treatments such as Priestley's are in the minority and most writers have had a good grasp of the meaning and implications of the "true" reincarnation theory—by which I mean the one most agreed on by religious and philosophic thought, the most logical, the most psychologically credible, and the most substantiated by fragmentary evidence.

For reasons of intellectual self-reassurance, then; for reasons of missionary material; and for reasons of psychological and philosophical insight, the survey of reincarnation as a theme in literature seems to me to be adequately justified. I would like therefore to discuss briefly some of the works in modern times in which reincarnation has figured prominently.

Before doing so, however, we need to raise this question. Does a writer always really believe in what he writes about? The question may seem to be one of academic interest only, but it is really of crucial significance if we are going to explore reincarnationist literature for the reenforcement of our own private convictions or of our missionary conversations. It is all very well to remark to an enthusiast of *Catcher in the Rye,* "Did you know that Salinger wrote a very fine short story about reincarnation?" But if he counters by saying: "Oh, Salinger couldn't really believe in that sort of thing"—and if you are not well informed in the matter—you find yourself at an embarrassing impasse. Therefore it is essential to give some thought to the relationship between what a man writes and what he really believes.

If we consider a type of writing that is very prevalent in

our time, namely advertising, I think we can see evidence in its most obvious form of the fact that the written word is not necessarily the equivalent of a writer's private convictions. An advertising man hires out his brains as other men hire out their muscles, and verbal facility, imagination, and style will enable him to write brilliantly effective ads without believing a word of what he has written.

Serious literature, to be sure, is a considerably different case, for the incentives of the writer are more personal and usually less crassly manipulative and commercial. But every creative act has its own complexities. A writer may write in a mood of fantasy what he does not seriously subscribe to, or he may use structural devices that are serviceable for his purpose but nothing more.

It is particularly necessary to weigh these possibilities when we consider a novel called *The Nazarene,* by Sholem Asch, which was published in 1939 and which was very widely read. This is a long, serious, and scholarly novel about the life and crucifixion of Jesus, and the very first paragraph of the book seems to strike at once a reincarnationist keynote. It reads as follows:

> Not the power to remember, but its very opposite, the power to forget, is a necessary condition of our existence. If the lore of the transmigration of souls is a true one, then these, between their exchange of bodies, must pass through the sea of forgetfulness. According to Jewish view we make the transition under the overlordship of the Angel of Forgetfulness. But it sometimes happens that the Angel of Forgetfulness himself forgets to remove from our memories the records of the former world; and then our senses are haunted by fragmentary recollections of another life.

The "Jewish view" that Asch refers to here is certainly not that of orthodox Judaism, which has nothing to say about reincarnation and would, in fact, repudiate it. But reincarnation does form an essential part of the Jewish Kabala—the secret teachings, it is said, of the Hebrew scriptures; of the Zohar, an ancient Kabalistic classic; and of the Hasidic movement of Jewish mystics which began in the eighteenth century and still exists.

In any case we seem to be well launched here into a re-incarnationist novel, and we do not have to read far to find our expectations confirmed. Pan Viadomsky, an old Polish scholar, accepts a young Jew as his assistant in the translation of an ancient Hebrew document which he has discovered. Before long the old man has confided in the young one his terrible secret: he remembers his past life in Jerusalem as a Roman official, and he is tormented by the memory of the part he played in the crucifixion of Jesus. He asks the young man to record his story, which the young man does; but in hearing it little by little he feels his own memories strangely stirred, for he too had lived before in the same period and the same place, and he too begins to feel compelled to write down in sequence the recollections that begin to inundate his consciousness. In addition, he helps Viadomsky translate the document which turns out to be the Gospel story as written by Judas Iscariot; and thus we have the story of Jesus told from the viewpoint of three different observers.

Of this, the editors wrote on the jacket of the book: "By an extraordinarily successful literary device Asch so tells his story that we see it from three different angles"; and I must confess that I believed, at first, that in calling this a "literary device" the editors were either willfully disguising Asch's serious philosophic intention, or else obtusely missing the point. More careful consideration of Asch's life and his other published work, however, has convinced me that they were in all probability completely right.

Every evidence that I now know of would seem to indicate that Asch was *not* a believer in reincarnation. A Polish Jew who wrote all his many novels in Yiddish, and who spent the last years of his life in the new state of Israel, Asch is reputed to have always carried with him a pocket-sized version of the Old Testament in Hebrew. This habit was indicative of his life-long absorption in Hebraic origins and values. In 1941, two years after the publication of *The Nazarene,* he wrote a book of non-fiction called *What I Believe.* The book was written at the time of the horrors of the Nazi persecution of Jews in Germany and from the preface of the book we can see that here was a man writing with a terrible sense of anguish and of urgency. If ever an articulate man had reason to speak words of truth as he saw it, for the sake of justifying the ways of God to man, or of man to man, Asch had that reason. Had he believed in a theory of human life that could very substantially give a rationale for the disaster that had overcome his people, and give cosmic perspective to those who had been so tragically swept up by it, now was the time to speak out. But in all the book there is no word of it. Not once is the word reincarnation mentioned or the theory even hinted at. In fact, exalting as it does a passionate faith in authority to which, in thoroughly orthodox tradition, he attaches a great deal of importance, the whole tenor of the book goes counter to such a belief.

An interesting case with which to compare Asch's *The Nazarene* is Somerset Maugham's *The Razor's Edge*. Published in 1943, *The Razor's Edge* had quite an impact on the reading public and undoubtedly had a far wider audience than did *The Nazarene* because it was made into a movie.

Viewers of the movie and perhaps the majority of the readers of the book found in it an interesting story about several vivid personalities, but most of them would be surprised to learn that the word reincarnation even occurs anywhere in the story. As a matter of fact it occurs only several times at the end of the book and not at all in the movie; and this may seem slight enough reason to consider the book in the category of reincarnationist fiction. But what was totally lost in the movie version, and what certainly was not apparent to hasty readers of the book (including many professional book reviewers) was that the whole point of the story hinges on the fact that young Larry Darrell, its hero, found the answer to the quest of his life in the Vedanta philosophy of India—a principal teaching of which is precisely the reincarnation concept.

In brief the story is this: Larry Darrell sees his best friend killed in the war, an event which affects him deeply. He becomes consumed with the desire to know why evil exists, if there is such a thing as God, and what happens to us, if anything, after we die.

Back in civilian life he is still obsessed by the same ques-

tions. Since he is endowed with a small annuity he chooses
—in Whitman's apt phrase—to loaf and invite his soul,
and shows no interest in bettering his worldly situation. In
fact, he refuses to accept job opportunities that present
themselves. But the girl he loves cannot marry him on
these terms. She breaks their engagement and marries a
wealthy young man whom she does not really love. Larry
goes to Paris and then to India, where he enters a spiritual
retreat known as an ashrama. Here he finds the answer to
his questions in the Vedanta philosophy and especially in
the discipline of meditation; and with his new insight
comes serenity, strength, and some minor power of healing
others of their physical ailments. Now at last he finds it
possible to return to life in America, and to work at a job,
any kind of job—driving a truck or a taxi, possibly—as
long as he can be in the midst of people and yet continue
to live a life of inner discipline.

At the end of the story he is asked the question: "Do you
believe in reincarnation?"—a question which, asked of a
convinced Vedantist, is almost like asking, of a convinced
Catholic, "Do you believe in the Virgin Birth?" But perhaps we must grant that a convert to either faith may have
reservations on one point or another. At any rate Larry re-
plies: "That's a very difficult question to answer. I don't
think it's possible for us Occidentals to believe in it as implicitly as these Orientals do. It's in their blood and bones.
With us it can only be an opinion. I neither believe in it
nor disbelieve in it." But he confesses to having had a curious experience one night while meditating on the flame of
a candle: he saw a line of human figures, one behind the

other, with each of whom he felt a sense of identity, as if they were his own former selves.

If the point is raised: did Maugham himself believe in reincarnation? we find that we are faced with an interesting dilemma.

There is nothing in any of his other novels or short stories that I know of that gives any indication of such a belief or even of such an interest. Like Asch, Maugham wrote a book of non-fiction that is the expression of his credo as an artist and as a man. It is called *The Summing Up*. In this book he admits to his preoccupation with the problem of evil and says, significantly, I think, that the only explanation of evil that appealed equally to his sensibility and his imagination and that could make the multitudinous tragedies of life bearable was the doctrine of reincarnation and karma. But, after a long paragraph discussing the reasonability of this point of view, he concludes: "I can only regret that I find the doctrine . . . impossible to believe. . . ."

This was written in 1938. Five years later in 1943 he wrote *The Razor's Edge*. Are we to surmise that in those five years he changed his mind, and came to a real belief in the theory of reincarnation? Or are we to infer that Larry's evasive: "I don't believe and I don't disbelieve" is an accurate reflection of Maugham's continuing agnosticism?

I for one have no definitive answer to the question. And yet I would tend to believe what I cannot prove—namely, that Maugham *did* come to believe it. It is difficult for me to believe that a man of as much irony and sophistication as Maugham would have even bothered to write as long,

as serious, as thoughtful, and as carefully written a book as
The Razor's Edge if he did not have some very strong feelings about the importance of the subject matter. Writing,
after all, entails considerable labor. Damon Runyan's classic statement: "Writing is the easiest thing in the world to
do: all the words are in the dictionary and all you have
to do is find them and type them out in a straight line
. . ." represents what the average non-writer believes about
writing; but it just happens not to be the truth.

In *The Summing Up* Maugham wrote: "I do not seek
to persuade anybody." He did not believe that art should
serve the purposes of propaganda. His taste and restraint
as a writer would have made him shrink from making
Larry an obvious mouthpiece for a message. But it seems to
me more than likely that by indirection, by oblique suggestion rather than direct onslaught, Maugham wished to
leave in the reader's mind the thought that answers *are* to
be found in the meditational disciplines and the philosophical teachings of India.

And so—though Asch at the very beginning of his novel
affirms reincarnation and Maugham at the very end of his
novel disclaims it—I believe that in private reality Asch
never gave it a serious thought beyond how it could serve
his artistic purpose, whereas Maugham lived with the concept for a long time in very great earnest, and became
finally if not a 100 per cent at least an 85 per cent believer
in the theory, so to speak—the 15 per cent representing that
reasonable reservation which any intelligent person must
have who has not met with firsthand incontrovertible proof
of it. But, like many another 85 per cent or even 100 per

cent believer in the theory, he was then constrained by an understandable hesitation to commit himself openly to his belief. This was perhaps artistic restraint, as we have seen, but it may also have been the discretion of a man of the world who does not wish to be thought peculiar. . . .

II

Discretion, in fact, is an important factor to be considered in any survey of the reincarnation theme in Occidental literature; and historically speaking, it is not difficult to see why.

In Europe and the Americas there has been a centuries long tradition of rigid dogmatic theology. To differ from this state-endorsed orthodoxy in some periods meant torture or death in the Inquisitor's Chambers; in other periods, ostracism and disgrace; and in modern times—however lax, skeptical, and basically irreligious they may be—it still represents a real risk to social standing and job security.

To be sure the idea of reincarnation has been a minor part of the intellectual heritage of the West since the time of Plato, who is reputed to have learned the idea from the Egyptians. Plato's conception of the pre-existence of the soul, its dim remembrance of a former state, and the succession of lives on earth which it must experience, has affected countless thinkers of our civilization. The Platonic influence can be found in the poetry for example of Henry More, Milton, Coleridge, and Shelley, to name but a few. Another source of this reincarnation heritage is to be found in the writings of the Gnostics, the Neo-Platonists, and a number of the early Church Fathers.

But for many centuries these streams of thought flowed underground, so to speak, known and appreciated only to the scholarly or mystical few who found them out and took them seriously, and only by those of sufficient intellectual independence or spiritual insight not to be held in bondage to the prevailing doctrines of the official church. It was not until the second half of the nineteenth century that the reincarnation idea became more widely known to Western man through two fresh and independent currents of thought: the Theosophical Society, founded in 1875 by Madame Blavatsky and Colonel Olcott, and the newly translated scriptures of the East.

The basic book of the Theosophical Society was written by Helena Petrovna Blavatsky, a strange, eccentric, and remarkable woman. Its title was *The Secret Doctrine*, its subtitle, *The Synthesis of Science, Religion, and Philosophy;* and it was presumably written through her clairvoyant and clairaudient transmission of knowledge from intelligences superior to man. Published in 1888, it made statements about the existence of supernormal faculties in man such as telepathy and clairvoyance; the vast antiquity of mankind; the illusory nature of matter; the transmutability of the elements; the fact that space is not empty; and the idea that the basic reality of the universe is light. These ideas, along with many others, seemed like pretentious nonsense to her contemporaries, and it was no wonder that the work was mercilessly ridiculed. Moreover, she wrote in a forthright and powerful style, assailing, in the manner of

Tom Paine, the confusions and absurdities of religious orthodoxy, but compounding the crime by also exposing
some of the fallacies of nineteenth-century materialist science as well as some of the errors of interpretation of the
currently popular Spiritualist movement. It was inevitable
that she should make enemies on every hand who, like the
enemies of Tom Paine, published slanderous and scur-
rilous untruths about her.

But, though it continues to be fashionable to write disparagingly about Mme. Blavatsky, the fact is that many of
the things she said that were incomprehensible to nineteenth-century science have been confirmed by the science
of the twentieth century. Modern physicists have vindicated many of her seemingly preposterous statements
about matter, light, space, and energy. Anthropologists
have had to revise repeatedly their estimates as to the time
of mankind's first appearance on this planet, their current
figure of about a million and a half years ago being far from
her own figure of 18 million years, but at least beginning to
approach it. And recent developments in parapsychology
make it clear that the supernormal faculties she wrote about
and that she herself manifested are actual faculties of the
human psyche, amenable to experiment in laboratories. It
becomes clear that Mme. Blavatsky was not as much of a
charlatan as she appeared to her contemporaries; and all
nineteenth-century reports about her need to be carefully
sifted for elements of slander and malicious invention. A
serious reappraisal both of Mme. Blavatsky and of Theosophy is, in fact, very much in order at this time, as well as

a new and more respectful look at what they still have to offer to the world.

In 1875 what they had to offer was very little in the way of published material. *Isis Unveiled* did not appear until 1877; *The Secret Doctrine* was published in 1888, and *The Key to Theosophy* in 1889. But there were lectures and discussion groups along the lines of the basic objectives of the Society which, as then stated, were "to collect and diffuse a knowledge of the laws which govern the universe." Among these laws was, of course, that of reincarnation.

The Society grew slowly at first. *Isis Unveiled* and *The Secret Doctrine* were difficult reading; but *The Key to Theosophy*—a book in the form of questions and answers about the fundamental teachings and the purposes of the Society—was clear, direct, and forceful, and still remains one of the best books for an inquirer to begin with. In any case, difficult reading or not, these books made a profound appeal to many persons who found the prevailing materialism of the day stifling to both mind and spirit. There soon followed popularizations of the subject by Annie Besant, C. W. Leadbeater, Jinarajadasa, and others; and this growing body of literature reached countless persons of intelligence, culture, and talent all over the English-speaking world as well as in other countries where translations became available.

It is known, for example, that the Irish Literary Revival, with its harking back to Irish mythology and ancient traditional lore, was in large part a direct outgrowth of Theosophical inspiration. George Russell (Æ) and William

Butler Yeats, who were the leaders of that revival, were
also active members of the Dublin Lodge of the Theosophical Society. They both later dropped out of the Society, but
they remained Theosophists at heart and believers in reincarnation all their lives. Robert Browning was acquainted with Theosophical leaders and had long discussions with them in London. Thomas Edison was a member
of the Society and a close friend of Colonel Olcott. It becomes more and more evident to any student of the subject
that the chain reactions set off by Theosophical ideas have
affected both contemporary literature and human affairs to
an immeasurable extent.

The second new current bringing the reincarnation idea
to the West was the religious literature of the East, made
available for the first time in the languages of Europe.
Translations of various fragments of Hindu, Buddhist, and
Parsi religions began to appear here and there in Europe
from the early 1800's onwards. Finally, in the years between 1881 and 1910, a careful and comprehensive 50-
volume work called *The Sacred Books of the East* was published. Edited by Max Muller, the brilliant philologist
and Orientalist, this series included translations done by a
number of Oriental scholars, and comprised the texts of
Hinduism, Buddhism, Mohammedanism, the Parsi religion, Confucianism, and Taoism.

Schopenhauer had read one of the first Latin translations
of the Upanishads as early as 1818 and frankly acknowledged
that his own philosophical system was greatly indebted to
it. "I anticipate," he wrote "that the influence of Sanskrit
literature will not be less profound than the revival of

Greek in the 14th century"; and it would seem that the spiritual renaissance in the West that his comparison pointed to has already begun, and that future decades will still further vindicate his prediction.

Thus Western man gradually became aware of the great unsuspected storehouse of spiritual and philosophical riches in the East. The Chinese, Mohammedan, and Parsi texts said nothing concerning reincarnation. But the Hindu and Buddhist texts said much. They dealt, moreover, with all the fundamental problems of philosophy. Though subtle and abstruse, they offered a practical way of liberation from the delusions of this world; and they had a tremendously fructifying effect on many of the finest minds of the time. Emerson, Thoreau, and Bronson Alcott were some of the American intellectuals whose enthusiasm for the ideas of the Upanishads, the Rig-Veda, and the Bhagavad-Gita went so far as to take form in a movement called Transcendentalism. The Transcendentalists, in turn, through their writings or their personal influence affected the thinking of many thousands of others. A study of the works of the Transcendentalists shows almost inescapably that they came to believe in reincarnation as a consequence of their Eastern studies; or at least they became 85 per cent believers, or possibly even 95 per cent believers, in the same sense that Maugham seems to be.

Yet because of the still rigid theological thinking of their time, they, too, felt the necessity of observing caution in speaking about it. Emerson, to be sure, made some very definite statements in favor of reincarnation in his *Essays*, though this is not always immediately apparent because he never used the word "reincarnation"—the words "transmigration" or "metempsychosis" being more in vogue at the time.

For example, in his essay on Swedenborg (in *Representative Men*) he spoke about the intuition of genius as follows: "If one should ask the reason of this intuition, the solution would lead us into that property which Plato denoted as reminiscence and which is implied by the Brahmins in the tenet of Transmigration. The soul having been often born, or as the Hindus say, 'traveling the path of existence through thousands of births' . . . no wonder she is able to recollect, in regard to any one thing, what she formerly knew." Here, in some 70 or 80 circumambulatory words he has said what could in essence be reduced very simply to three, namely: reincarnation explains genius.

Emerson gave unmistakable assent to reincarnation in many other passages throughout his work. But he wrote with such indirection and subtlety, often in sentences so long and involved, so elliptically and poetically phrased, and so clothed in the language of classical allusion, that he was in little danger of being branded heretic because so few people could really know with certainty what he was talking about.

However, as he himself said in his essay on *Spiritual Laws*, "a man cannot bury his meanings so deep in his book but time and like-minded men will find them"; and it is with Emerson as it is with Plato, of whose works Aristotle wrote that they were both published and not published.

. . . The fact that reincarnation and karma were Emerson's frame of reference, and a tacit working assumption underlying much of what he wrote, becomes quite clear once one is alerted to the fact that he was thoroughly imbued with the Hindu point of view. It serves then to make clear many passages which otherwise are obscure, or in some instances downright nonsensical to a rational but uninformed mind.

We who live in the second half of the twentieth century have come a long way from the stuffy theological tyranny of the nineteenth. Discoveries in the fields of psychology, comparative religion, anthropology, linguistics, hypnosis, electronics, atomic energy, and space travel have expanded horizons in every direction. Evidence for the reality of reincarnation has appeared in many places and from many diverse sources, and it has been sufficiently strong to persuade many professional people—hitherto materialistic and skeptical—to a new point of view about the universe.

I personally know doctors, psychiatrists, engineers, ministers, and teachers who not only have an interest in reincarnation, but feel a genuine conviction about it. Yet they are still fearful about letting it be generally known, lest they lose their professional or social standing in the community. Writers are usually less dependent than other professional people on a salaried job; but they too must be careful not to alienate their public. The fact that in recent years two very fine books about reincarnation have appeared under assumed names, one in England and one in this country, is, I think, significant.

And so we must recognize two factors with regard to the literary treatment of reincarnation in the Western Hemisphere, one on either side of the ledger:

1) A writer may have no belief in reincarnation at all, but use it purely as a convenient literary device; and

2) A writer may have a very strong leaning toward, or a very deep conviction about, reincarnation; but, for fear of public derision, disguise his true feelings under the cloak of fantasy or agnosticism.

It is my considered opinion that most Western writers who have dealt with reincarnation fall into the second category, and only a very small minority into the first.

III

With these considerations clearly in mind, we can more fairly approach the literature of reincarnation, which exists in far greater abundance than one might imagine. A mere enumeration of all the titles of poetry, plays, short stories, and novels in which reincarnation prominently figures would, in fact, fill many pages and become quite tedious reading. I shall refer here, therefore, only to a few examples which to me for one reason or another have particular interest, and which seem to me would lead others to pleasurable exploratory journeys.

In the realm of poetry literally hundreds of reincarnationist passages have been penned by major and minor poets of English literature for several centuries. "I hold

that when a person dies/His soul returns again to earth;
Arrayed in some new flesh disguise/Another mother gives
him birth," wrote John Masefield in *A Creed*. "They will
come back, come back again, as long as the red Earth
rolls./He never wasted a leaf or a tree. Do you think
He would squander souls?" wrote Rudyard Kipling in
Naulahka. They are two much-quoted passages. "When
you were a tadpole and I was a fish in the Paleozoic time"
are the opening lines of a well-known poem by Langdon
Smith. Though entitled "Evolution" it should more properly have been called "Reincarnation" [1] and its popularity
may be due to the fact that it is a love poem, written in a
light and charming vein by a man to the girl he claims to
have loved throughout their many incarnations.

I shall forego citing any other poetic lines here, however;
an interested reader can easily find them in E. D. Walker's
anthology[2] or in the more recent anthology of Head and
Cranston.[3]

Particularly worth noting, I feel, are poets Robert

1 "When you were a tadpole and I was a fish
     In the Paleozoic time,
  And side by side on the ebbing tide
     We sprawled through the ooze and slime,
  Or skittered with many a caudal flip
     Through the depths of the Cambrian fen,
  My heart was rife with the joy of life,
     For I loved you even then."

In *The Best Loved Poems of the American People*, selected by Hazel
Felleman (Garden City Publishing Co., N.Y., 1936).
2 *Reincarnation*, E. D. Walker (The Aryan Philosophical Press, Pt. Loma,
Calif., 1923).
3 *Reincarnation, An East-West Anthology*, J. Head and S. L. Cranston
(The Julian Press, N.Y., 1961).

Browning and Walt Whitman, both of whom seem to have been convinced believers in the theory, and in both of whose works a number of very pointed and eloquent lines on the subject can be found. I should like also to call attention to Kahlil Gibran, perhaps the most widely loved poet of modern times, who, according to his friend and biographer Barbara Young, also believed that the soul returned many times to earth.[4] There are only a few lines at the end of his masterpiece, *The Prophet,* that give any explicit indication of this. Almustafa the Prophet, in taking leave of the people of Orphalese, says:

> *Forget not that I shall come back to you.*
> *A little while, and my longing shall gather dust and foam for another body.*
> *A little while, a moment of rest upon the wind, and another woman shall bear me.*

There are a few other lines scattered here and there in Gibran's work which are equally explicit. But the reincarnation perspective is implicit throughout his poetry; it suffuses it, in fact, as the flavor of anise suffuses a cake—distinctive, unmistakable, and unsubtractable. The wisdom of his books can certainly be appreciated and practiced by people whether they accept reincarnation or not. But, as with the works of Emerson, much of it must remain strange or even unintelligible unless one recognizes the esoteric perspective from which it was written.

There seem to have been far fewer dramas than poems written with reincarnationist content—possibly because

[4] *This Man from Lebanon,* Barbara Young (Alfred Knopf, N.Y., 1945).

playwrights are more dependent on immediate public acceptance than poets, and cannot always hope to carry off what must seem like mere fantasy or superstition to the average mind of our times. The idea does lend itself to dramatic treatment, however, and it has been used in *The Adding Machine*,[5] *The Road to Yesterday*,[6] and an unfortunate play called *The Ladder* which a Texas millionaire, an ardent reincarnationist, financed for two years on Broadway despite the fact that the public showed no interest. He finally made admission free to anyone who wanted to come.

Richard Wagner became much interested in Buddhism and Eastern thought generally and certain passages in his letters indicate that he came to accept reincarnation as the only possible explanation for the tragedy of human life. So strongly did he feel this that he wrote a reincarnationist musical drama called *Die Sieger* (The Victor) but the work was never completed and some of it was later incorporated into *Parsifal*.

Generally speaking, we find with plays what we also find with novels on the subject: sometimes reincarnation is just talked about by the characters; sometimes it is an essential part of the structure of the story. The difference can be clearly seen by contrasting two successful plays, one American and one European: *The Return of Peter Grimm*[7] and *The Master of Palmyra*.

The Return of Peter Grimm was written by David Be-

5 By Elmer Rice.
6 By B. M. Dix and E. G. Sutherland (Samuel French, publishers, N.Y., 1925).
7 In *Six Plays*, David Belasco (Little Brown and Co., Boston, 1929).

lasco and produced in New York City in 1911. Belasco, a
noted playwright and producer, had had since early youth
many curious psychic experiences of his own, which led
him to a study of spiritualism and psychical research. The
play tells the story of a kindly but obstinate old man, Peter
Grimm, who has exacted a death-bed promise from a young
woman that she will marry his nephew. After death Grimm
realizes what a scoundrel the nephew really is, and he returns—in spirit form—to try to avert the marriage. His
presence is finally sensed by the living, and he accomplishes
his objective.

Structurally, then, this could be called a spiritualist play
since its outcome depends on the fact of Grimm's return
in spirit form after death. However it does contain a very
interesting reincarnationist passage between Grimm and
his doctor. The doctor, knowing that the old man has only
a short time to live, and being himself a student of psychical research, has suggested that they make a pact: the first
to die shall try to come back and make his presence known
to the other. Grimm scoffs at this, saying: "No, Andrew,
no. Positively no. I refuse. Don't count on *me* for any assistance in your spook tests." To which the doctor answers:
"And how many times do you think *you've* been a spook
yourself? You can't tell me that man is perfect; that he
doesn't live more than one life; that the soul doesn't go on
and on. Pshaw! The persistent personal energy *must* continue, or what *is* God?"

This passage shows that Belasco probably had an interest in reincarnation as well as in psychic research—an inference that would seem borne out by the fact that he gave

a reincarnationist interpretation to the legend of the Flying Dutchman in his play called *Van Der Decken*. It is also interesting for its use of the phrase "persistent personal energy"—a phrase which may be more congenial to some minds than the word "soul," which has so many unfortunate connotations to those who dislike traditional thinking.

In marked contrast to this play, in which reincarnation is only referred to, we find in *The Master of Palmyra*[8] by Wilbrandt a play that is structurally dependent on the reincarnation idea. I am acquainted with the play only through Mark Twain's description of it; I do not know if it is still ever presented on the boards at this late date, but I would certainly doubt it. According to Twain's enthusiastic description, it was a highly effective play, repeated for many years in Berlin and in Vienna, with the most profound effect upon the spectators. It showed five successive lifetimes of the same individual, four times as a woman and once as a man, the five characters being played by the same actress. It also showed a young man named Apelles who has been granted deathless life by the Spirit of Life, and who is present as a young and handsome man throughout the five incarnations of the other. He lives to regret his gift of eternal life and youth in the same body, and finally prays to be released from it.

One of the chief fascinations of the play, according to Twain, lay in watching the artistry of the actress who in each succeeding incarnation showed the subtle and unconscious strands of character that came from each of the pre-

8 "About Play-Acting," in *The Man Who Corrupted Hadleyburg* (Mark Twain, Harper & Bros., N.Y., 1917).

ceding ones. Finally a beautiful fruition and distillation of all the previous experiences was seen in the last incarnation as Zenobia, a woman of great compassion for all who suffer.

The notion of presenting a sequence of lives of a given individual has been used by several novelists, as for example A. E. W. Mason who gave three successive incarnations in *The Three Gentlemen*,[9] and Warwick Deeping who showed four successive ones in *I Live Again*.[10] In both cases there was some indication of psychological growth from life to life, and of dim stirrings of memory of the previous ones, though *I Live Again* seems to me to be by far the better novel. In other treatments we find a present personality remembering or reliving fragments of three or four previous lives. A notable example of this is to be found in Jack London's *The Star Rover*,[11] in which a prisoner at San Quentin manages during the excruciating pain of the strait jacket to release his mind from his body, and in this state relives a number of previous incarnations. This type of approach is also used by Rudyard Kipling in his short story "The Greatest Story in the World," [12] in which a young man has spontaneous flashes of memory of several previous lives.

In other works of fiction the writer limits himself to a canvas of two lives only, with their emotional or psychological interrelationship. Usually it is a love intrigue or a frustrated love that forms the pivot of the story, and the theme has been handled in a great variety of ways. For example

9 (Doubleday, Doran and Co., N.Y., 1932).
10 (Alfred Knopf, N.Y., 1942).
11 (The Macmillan Co., N.Y., 1919).
12 In *Many Inventions* (Doubleday, Page, and Co., 1922).

in *She*,[13] by Rider Haggard, there is conscious memory of the past life on the part of the woman because, having bathed periodically in a supernatural Flame of Life deep in an underground African cave, she has been alive and beautiful for all the intervening centuries. *She* is perhaps the best known of Rider Haggard's many fantastic romances, and it has exercised a strange fascination over several generations of readers, including many distinguished men of letters. It has been made into a movie several times, and probably will be again. Haggard was a firm believer in reincarnation, as all his biographers point out, and he was convinced that he had been a Norseman, a Zulu, and an Egyptian in previous lives.

A more contemporary and realistic treatment of a two-life romance is found in *Flight from Youth* [14] by William E. Barrett. In this rather fascinating story a young man who has never studied flying feels the strange impulse one day to walk out on a flying field, enter a plane, and fly it. He knows instinctively what to do in the air, and suddenly he is invaded by a rush of vivid and detailed memory pictures of a previous life, in which as an English aviator over France he was shot down by a German plane. He had left the girl he loved in England; and he feels now that she must still be alive and that he must find her. This he succeeds in doing; and he also succeeds in proving his identity to her by relating to her the intimate conversations and the incidents of their previous romance. She is now almost twenty years his senior, and in the interim she has been

13 (Books, Inc., N.Y., 1887).
14 (Doubleday and Co., N.Y., 1960).

very unhappily married. But they feel the same strong spiritual kinship and physical attraction that they had felt before, and at the end of the story they marry again.

Perhaps the most provocative story of recent years on the reincarnation theme, and one of the most deftly handled, is a short story by J. D. Salinger called "Teddy." [15]

Teddy is a ten-year-old American boy who spends part of every day in meditation. He has some unusual capacities for clairvoyance and precognition, and he clearly remembers his past life as a Hindu yogi. As with other Salinger stories, this one presents an interesting and dramatic incident rather than a complicated plot; but the treatment combines an acutely sensitive description of physical detail with an acutely sensitive awareness of philosophical overtones. Salinger is notoriously secretive about himself and his affairs, and there is nothing in print that I know of that would prove him to be a believer in reincarnation. But it is known that he has been a student both of yoga and of Zen Buddhism, and the content of this story would lead me to believe that it could hardly have been written by one who did not have an expanded view of human life.

In Salinger's story reincarnation is merely talked about; but Teddy's casual attitude toward death—even the immediate possibility of his own—is directly related to his complete assurance that death is really not the end of life. "It's so silly," he says. "All you do is get the heck out of your body, when you die. My gosh, everybody's done it thousands and thousands of times. Just because they don't remember it doesn't mean they haven't done it. It's so silly."

[15] *Nine Stories* (Little, Brown and Co., Boston, 1948).

And this leads us to make another distinction. We have already noted that there are fictional treatments in which reincarnation is a structural element of the story, and those in which it is merely talked about by some of the characters. We can now observe that the talk may range from a few remarks by a character—tentatively and almost apologetically made, the subject being dropped like a prickly cactus immediately thereafter by the author (as in Tolstoi's *War and Peace*, James Jones' *From Here to Eternity*, and Tom Chamales' *Never So Few*)—to the statements made positively by a character (like Teddy) who unabashedly believes in reincarnation; who has something original or significant to say about it; and whose actions in some way both reflect this philosophical point of view and influence the outcome of the story.

There exists a whole minor genre of fiction, in fact, which is written from the standpoint of a definite commitment to the reincarnation outlook, or—strictly speaking—to the esoteric outlook of which reincarnation forms an essential part. This fiction is often amateurishly done, and partly for this reason and partly because of the nature of its subject matter, it is not well known to the general public. It has its own special following, however, and despite its conspicuous literary limitations it sometimes makes a valuable contribution in that it brings philosophic knowledge to people who, without the sugar coating of a story, might never come to appreciate it.

The novels of Cyril Scott and L. Adams Beck fall into this latter category. Cyril Scott's *The Initiate*, *The Initiate in the New World*, and *The Initiate in the Dark*

Cycle are all very flimsy as regards story or dramatic interest; yet the conversation of the central character, the Initiate, on matters ranging through sex, karma, morality, Krishnamurti, jealousy, clairvoyance, and many other themes, is of absorbing interest, at least to one seeking to reappraise life in terms of a more expanded cosmic outlook.

L. Adams Beck was one of three pseudonyms used by a woman who spent much time in the Orient and who studied Eastern religions extensively. Under the name of E. Barrington she wrote a number of historical novels which had considerable success when they first appeared; but it is her two novels on Oriental philosophy, *The House of Fulfillment* and *The Garden of Vision,* which continue to be of interest to students of the esoteric, even though first published in the 1920's. Both are love stories and I suppose one might call them spiritual love stories in the sense that both partners to the romance are on a spiritual quest involving the disciplines of yoga or of zen. If the reader himself feels an absorbing interest in such a spiritual quest he may find much here of significance and value; if not, he will undoubtedly find both these books extremely dull reading.

Another writer who was frankly committed to the point of view of Eastern philosophy, including reincarnation, was Talbot Mundy. Mundy spent many years in the British government service in India and Eastern Africa, and wrote some thirty-five adventure novels, most of them laid in the Orient and dealing with some aspect of Oriental thought. *Om, the Secret of Ahbor Valley,* is one of the most interesting from the point of view of reincarnation and occult philosophy. Mundy was a Theosophist and a student of Mme. Blavatsky's *Secret Doctrine*. The book *Om* was, in fact, written at the Theosophical headquarters that was once located at Point Loma, California. In another book of non-fiction called *I Say Sunrise* Mundy has an excellent chapter in which he frankly discusses his own belief in reincarnation.

IV

I think it will be seen even from this brief survey that reincarnation has stirred the interest of a great many writers, and that the topic has been handled in a wide variety of ways. The possibilities of the subject, however, have by no means been exhausted.

There has never been an opera, for example, on the reincarnation theme, and such an opera could be very powerful. Richard Wagner started to write one, and his plan was to have "the previous life of the leading characters merge into the present existence by means of an accompanying musical reminiscence";[16] but as we have already pointed out he gave up the notion and incorporated most of this musical material into another work.

To my knowledge, also, there have been very few humorous treatments of reincarnation, although the theme holds tremendous comic potentials. Don Marquis' amusing *Archy and Mehitabel* [17] dealt with the reappearance of poet François Villon in the body of Archy, the office cockroach

16 *Collected Writings* (Kapp ed.); VI, 278.
17 (Doubleday, Doran and Co., N.Y., 1932).

who wrote free verse on the typewriter, and of Cleopatra in the body of the disreputable cat Mehitabel; but this belongs more properly in the category of transmigration than reincarnationist fiction. *The Cat Who Saw God* [18] is a novel done with a light touch; but this, again, deals with transmigration—in this case, of the soul of the Emperor Nero into the body of a cat for purposes of moral redemption.

Bunker Bean[19] is the only comic novel that I know of that deals with reincarnation proper. In this book, Bunker Bean's innocent faith that he is the reincarnation of Napoleon and of an ancient Egyptian king is the means of transforming him from a fearful and inhibited young man into a self-confident captain of finance. He learns in the end that the clairvoyant who told him of these glorious past lives was only a fraud; and he also learns that it is not really necessary to believe in past grandeurs to live successfully now—that as a man thinketh in his heart, so is he. The point is certainly well taken. But *Bunker Bean* was written many years ago, before the time even of woman suffrage, and its humor seems a bit clumpish and out of date to the modern reader.

Some contemporary light-hearted treatments of reincarnation would, therefore, be a welcome addition to the library, and might help give perspective to those who tend to take the subject too ponderously.

But apart from the fact that there are several unworked literary areas, the potentials of reincarnation as thematic material are great because we are only at the threshold—

[18] By Anna Gordon Keown (Wm. Morrow, N.Y., 1932).
[19] Harry Leon Wilson (the Curtis Publishing Co., 1912).

in my considered opinion—of the scientific substantiation of the hypothesis.

Up until now writers who have wanted to write about reincarnation have been circumscribed by a public opinion which most of them have feared to offend. If by the end of the twentieth century the reincarnation theory is as well established in the minds of educated people as the theory of evolution was at the end of the nineteenth, then writers will no longer need to tread warily with their subject—writing prefaces that confess to their proclivity to fantasy, or autobiographical essays that disclaim any serious belief in what they write about. . . .

Moreover, writers on reincarnation have in the past been handicapped by lack of psychologically precise information regarding a theory which to them at most seemed logically and philosophically reasonable. They have followed therefore the general outlines of Theosophical textbooks or the suggestive material available in the religions of the East—excellent sources, both of them, but in many respects vague and sometimes even misleading.

The new knowledge provided by several branches of psychology, particularly as regards hypnosis and the mechanisms of the unconscious mind, now illumines much in reincarnationist psychology, and can provide authors with a deepened insight into that vast portion of the unconscious mind that goes far beyond birth. In addition, the case history data from the files of the great American clairvoyant Edgar Cayce has in recent years been made available to the public; and while this data may not be regarded by all people as being scientifically acceptable, it does at least offer much suggestive material that is new and, for those who can accept it, enriches the idea of karmic law with many psychological and ethical insights.

If other research sources in the future will confirm and enlarge upon the Cayce data—and I am inclined to feel that they will—writers will have a tremendous storehouse of material on which to draw for plots, psychological analyses, and for the strange and intricate operations of destiny.

The case of Émile Zola is interesting in this connection. Writing in the second half of the nineteenth century, Zola was much affected by the science and philosophical determinism of his time. He had profound sympathy for the poor and the oppressed and, like Balzac before him, set himself the task of presenting accurate and all-encompassing studies of human society. His avowed purpose was to reveal the need for broad social and economic reforms, and he devoted twenty-five years of his life to the writing of twenty interrelated books called the Rougon-Maquart series. He was particularly preoccupied with the idea of heredity, and the novels show the gradual degeneracy of five generations of the Rougon and Maquart family, all the members of which were somehow touched by a hereditary taint.

In this work Zola founded the movement of literary Naturalism, and, though the books were not great popular successes, like his later work *Nana,* they were none the less widely read. And yet—great as was his literary and humanitarian accomplishment—he was limited by the scientific notions of his time. If reincarnation is finally established as a scientific truth it will be seen that his thesis was very inadequate to the truth of the matter. For the principle of karma underlies both heredity and environment. By the reincarnationist view, heredity and environment are not denied. They are unquestionably determinants of the human condition. But they are partial and secondary determinants, since they both are the manifestation of karmic law.

Thus the reincarnation idea opens the portals of a vaster, subtler, and still more awesome spectacle of human life than that visible by nineteenth-century man. Perhaps some master of fiction will appear in the coming generation, some new Zola or Balzac, who will feel for this idea the same excitement and missionary passion that Zola felt for the idea of heredity and Balzac for the vast human tragicomedy. Instead of showing five generations of a single family, he may choose to show five or more lifetimes of the same group of sinning and sinned against souls, with all the complicated psychological and karmic interrelationships between them. It would certainly be a canvas of great magnitude, and it could engender not only great dramatic excitement but profound philosophical insight into the operations of life.

It is certainly likely that, once reincarnation is established scientifically, many writers will avail themselves of the theme. Flashbacks to previous lives may become quite common and experimental work in different fields can provide the basis for a variety of flashback techniques: hypnotic regression, LSD and mushroom experiences. We may have a whole new literary rash of reincarnationist fiction, including family sagas, historical trilogies, and multi-layered psychoanalyses that will make all sagas, trilogies, and psychological probings up to now seem paltry by comparison.

And then perhaps the public and the writers themselves will begin to tire of such vast canvases and such intricate subconscious delvings. Perhaps then new writers will appear who—instead of ponderous accumulative lifetimes or ingenious flashbacks to one or more lifetimes—will confine themselves to small vignettes of one life only. Perhaps finally, since everybody will know the truth of reincarnation anyway and it can be taken completely for granted, they will only lightly refer to it, here and there, in jest, in passing, even as it is lightly referred to in many books of the East, and even as it seems to be referred to here and there in our Christian Bible.

And then—assuming that all the voluminously explicit reincarnationist books have been destroyed, as well they might be by future cataclysms, future monarchs, or future religious fanatics of the one-life persuasion—it may well be that future civilizations, finding the latter-day books, and noting these light and passing reincarnationist references, will wonder about them. Perhaps their translators of dead languages will, finding the strange passages, delete them for being so absurd; or force their meaning into other meanings, with footnotes of explanatory matter. Or perhaps the translators will leave the passages alone, and the scholars will, according to the prevailing philosophy of the age, refer to them either as childish relics of an earlier mythology, or as marvelous intuitions of the truth on the part of the barbarous ancients of the late twentieth century.

And so we see there might well be truth in the cyclic notion, for it is quite conceivable that the wheel of civilizations will turn from Ignorance to Knowledge and back to Ignorance again.

But let us not forget that these vast cycles are not mathematically rigid, nor eternally repetitive as regards the souls who experience them. For mind evolves onward, through and beyond the civilization cycles that nurture mankind; and new souls pass through these experiences even as new pupils keep passing through the annually repeated classes in a grammar school; and all of life is meant for the ever-widening expansion of consciousness.

7

OUR LITTLE BROTHERS
Reincarnation and Animals

I

When Charles Darwin published his theory of evolution in 1859 it became almost overnight the sensation of the century. Few books have caused so much excitement, so much animosity, and so much controversy as *The Origin of the Species*. Thousands of pious persons were deeply perturbed by it; all over the world religious prelates were roused to fury. And in the heated debates, public and private, that were part of the universal scientific and theological storm, the subject naturally gave rise to much ill-natured and good-natured humor as to the apes in other people's ancestry. "Is it through your grandfather or your grandmother that you claim descent from a monkey?" Thomas Huxley was sarcastically asked, in public debate, by Bishop Wilberforce. . . .

The theory of reincarnation has not yet been brought to public attention on the authority of evidences convincingly phalanxed by some important scientist; but it probably will be before very long, and at that time we can expect a similar thing to happen. It will be fearfully and suspiciously rejected by the orthodox, furiously attacked by churchmen, and endlessly joked about by everybody else —and one of the major themes of the jokes will probably

depend on the usual confusion of reincarnation with transmigration, or the idea that after death we may come back
to earth as animals.

"I've been reading about reincarnation," one comedian
has already said, "and now I'm worried. I'm afraid I'll
come back as a jackass." "Don't worry," came the answer.
"The same thing couldn't happen twice." This is the sort
of thing that we can expect—until, that is, people become
sufficiently enlightened to know that reincarnation means
evolution and that in the normal course of the evolutionary process life goes forward to successively higher forms
rather than regresses backward to lower ones. There are
some groups of reincarnationists, to be sure, who maintain
that debased and bestial human beings do sometimes come
back as animals;[1] but even they usually admit that this happens only in exceptional cases.

I personally feel, with the majority of reincarnationists,
that human beings do *not* revert to the animal kingdom.
Minor retrogressions are always possible within the human
realm; but—just as there is a valve in the heart that prevents the flow of the blood backwards—there may be a
comparable mechanism in nature that prevents a reversion
from a higher kingdom to a lower one.

Why so many people are revolted at the thought of becoming an animal, or amused at the thought of imputing
such a transformation to somebody else, is in itself a fascinating question. In part it may be due to an unconscious
repudiation of our own animal nature, in part to that sense

1 As for example the Sat Sang group. See *The Path of the Masters,* Julian
Johnson, M.D. (Sawan Service League, Panjab, India).

of pride and superiority that is so distinctive of the human
species. Whatever the underlying reason, the aversion to
animals coexists in human nature with another and con-
tradictory attitude toward them, namely, a deep and enduring affection. And among those who feel this affection
strongly, there is an important question that inevitably
arises in connection with reincarnation, as soon as the ini-
tial shock of the idea has worn off. That question is: Do
animals reincarnate too?

I confess that I would like to answer the question with a
resounding affirmative, if only because I have had a number of four-footed friends whom I would like very much to
meet again. But I must admit that I have no scientific justification for so positive an assertion. There are many kinds
of circumstantial evidence that point to the reincarnation
of human beings, but there is none that I know of that
substantiates animal reincarnation.

However, though empirical evidence is lacking, logic
and inference would seem to make a rather strong case—
at least for those who find the reincarnation principle itself
logically and inferentially acceptable. It would hardly seem
likely that only one class of life, the human, is making purposive advances upward, and all other classes of life are
merely static props to the human drama. All other classes
of life do seem to participate in a dynamic evolutionary
process, and there are a great number of structural and biological similarities between the various kingdoms. It is far
more logical, therefore, to infer that there is one far-off
divine event, as Tennyson put it, toward which *the whole
creation* moves.

In questions of this kind I personally find it interesting to turn to the materials of the Theosophical Society. Theosophy affirmed the reality of reincarnation long before there were any appearances of evidence anywhere, and it is worth noting therefore that they affirmed it to be a *universal principle,* which applies not only to human beings but to all life units, or monads, and all centers of consciousness everywhere.[2] All life came from the same great Central Source, and all life is traveling, they say, on a long evolutionary pilgrimage back to that Source. Broadly speaking, life evolves from the mineral kingdom to the plant, from the plant to the animal, from the animal to the human, and from the human to the near-divine and then the divine.

This seems philosophically reasonable, and I for one am willing to give the idea tentative acceptance at least. But there are a good many questions that come to mind as soon as one starts to speculate on the specific mechanism of the whole operation. These difficulties are similar to those that have confronted evolutionists in their efforts to classify the multitudinous life forms that exist on this planet, and to discern on what lines the ascent—or the descent—of the evolutionary procession takes place.

Granting that each little life unit re-embodies, one cannot help wondering as to the future destiny of many famil-

2 More exactly, they consider human reincarnation to be a special case of the more general principle of *re-embodiment.* This would seem to be a mere verbal quibble, except for the fact that the *carne* of reincarnation does mean *flesh,* whereas to re-embody means to come back into another form or body, whether of flesh or not, and hence can include other types of life such as mineral and plant. See *The Divine Plan,* by Geoffrey A. Baborka (Theosophical Publishing House, Adyar, Madras, India, 1961), pp. 25-26.

iar forms. What becomes of an onion, for example, in its next succeeding embodiment? And what can a graduate petunia aspire to? Does the plant that has perfected its character next become a tree? And if so, which tree? and why? That lions might become house cats in some future incarnation, or mountain wolves be dogs, seems a neat enough progression; but what do electric eels come back as? and koala bears? and fleas? and the duck-billed platypus? I can find no specific answers to these questions, not even in Theosophical literature; and I must confess that, even if I were to find them, I might still be dubious about them. There is something so inherently strange about life and so mysterious about all its transformations.

Questions of this type, however, are not likely to stir any great excitement in most people's minds. But there is another question about animals that often generates considerable heat, and that is this: Do animals finally become human beings?

Before we can answer this question I think we must realize that in common speech we usually use the word *animal* to refer to any four-footed creature. More strictly speaking, however, *animal* includes any living organism capable of moving about, and incapable of making its own food by photosynthesis. In this larger sense, then, protozoa, sponges, worms, fish, reptiles, insects, and birds are all animals; and to assume that they all finally re-embody as human beings is to make a rather large assumption.

The assumption has its difficulties, too, since structurally speaking many of these forms seem unrelated. Evolutionists have regarded molluscs and sponges, I believe, as two side developments that never gave rise to other animals. The insect world also seems to be a separate branch on the evolutionary tree of life, culminating in bees, ants, and butterflies but leading to no higher form. Birds and mammalian animals apparently come from the same common ancestor; but the mammals culminated in man, whereas the birds remained birds, which may have been rather clever of them.

If we turn again to Theosophy, we find some very interesting statements in this connection. Theosophy affirms that there is not only one evolutionary stream on this planet, but several parallel streams, only one of them culminating in the human kingdom, and the others culminating in equally high forms called Devas but not visible to normal human sight. Birds, for example, are supposed to be on a different evolutionary line from our own, and they become nature spirits and devas rather than human beings. Our own ascent arose along this line: minerals, mosses, ferns, flowering plants, shrubs, trees; antediluvian reptiles on one hand and lower mammals on the other; thence to mammals, domestic animals, primitive men, ordinary men, and advanced men of the human kingdom. Still another line of ascent is: minerals, grasses, cereals, ants, bees, tiny etheric creatures, surface fairies, fire spirits, astral sylphs, astral devas and higher devas.[3]

All of this may or may not be true. It is fascinating but,

3 Diagram 6, pp. 98-99, *Where Theosophy and Science Meet,* Part III, ed. by D. D. Kanga (The Adyar Library Assn., Adyar, Madras, India, 1939). See also *The Hidden Side of Things,* Lines of Evolution, C. W. Leadbeater (The Theosophical Publishing House, Adyar, Madras, India, 1913), p. 117.

in the present stage of science at least, undemonstrable.
Why a cereal should become an ant is certainly no clearer
to me than why a fern should become a flowering plant.
But then neither is it clear to me why a caterpillar should
become a butterfly. Some people may raise amused eye-
brows at the fairy, sylph, and deva evolutions, but I personally find nothing instrinsically illogical about it and
much that is refreshingly new. The idea has the merit at
least of expanding the narrow confines of our usual complacency by causing us to recognize that other life streams
may exist, just as significant and important as our own.

On the other hand, the Theosophists make another
statement about animals about which I have always had
serious reservations, namely, their notion of the animal
"group soul."

This is the idea that after death, the souls of animals
are soon drawn into a kind of bucket full of other animal
souls of the same species. When the time comes for new
animals of the same species to be born, soul substance is
poured out of the bucket, so to speak, into new animal
bodies, but no individuality persists. The accumulated
experiences of each animal contribute to the pool, however,
and affect the intelligence and capacity of the new out-
pouring. Finally the time comes when the higher animals
such as dogs, cats, elephants, horses, and monkeys are in a
pool so advanced that the animals in it "individualize" as
a human being.[4]

To this whole "pool of souls" idea my unregenerate

[4] *Man Visible and Invisible,* C. W. Leadbeater (The Theosophical Publishing House, Adyar, Madras, India, 1959), p. 35.

impulse is to say *stuff and nonsense.* I find the notion inherently implausible, and essentially contrary to the whole idea of evolving monads of life.

I can conceive of a guiding spirit, so to speak, for every species of animals, which somehow directs its destiny. And I can see that animals might have a group spirit or group consciousness in the same way that musicians and plumbers, Muslims and Seventh Day Adventists might be said to have a group consciousness, because their thoughts tend to run in the same channels. But both of these concepts are quite different from what Leadbeater describes with his patronizing buckets and ponds and pools.

To assume further that only human beings have "individuality" and animals have to attain to it seems to me to be on a par with the widespread notion of the white man that "all Chinese look alike" (matched by the Chinese notion, no doubt, that all white men look alike) and is indicative (I think) of an indiscriminating and imperfect observation of animals who, as any animal lover will tell you, have noticeably unique personalities, even at a very early age.[5] Moreover, I find no mention of the group-soul idea in the basic Theosophical writings of Mme. Blavatsky —which, after all, have been vindicated on many other points—and I see no reason to believe it just because Annie Besant and C. W. Leadbeater said it was so. Both of

---

[5] Darwin makes mention of the wide variability of the faculties of individuals of the same animal species in chapter 3 of *The Descent of Man.* "I have found on frequent enquiry that it is the unanimous opinion of all those who have long attended to animals of many kinds, including birds, that *the individuals differ greatly in every mental characteristic.*" (Modern Library ed.), p. 446.

them wrote extensively and with great positiveness on the matter, presumably on the basis of Mr. Leadbeater's clairvoyance. But any clairvoyant can be wrong and very often is, and there is good reason to be doubtful of some of Mr. Leadbeater's clairvoyant perceptions. This is not only because they have lacked evidential substantiations but also because they have sometimes been proven completely or partially wrong. Besant and Leadbeater predicted, for example, on the basis of the latter's clairvoyance, that Jeddu Krishnamurti, a young Hindu boy, was destined to become the new Christ and the new World Teacher, and they went so far as to begin selecting twelve apostles for his retinue; but, though Mr. Krishnamurti has become a writer and teacher of considerable stature in the world, he himself repudiated the role of Messiah and also the entire Theosophic teaching, much to the embarrassment of everyone concerned.

I trust that my Theosophical friends will forgive me for bringing to mind these delicate matters. It is done, not with malice, but with concern that some Theosophists have had the tendency to believe too slavishly in their literature without any substantiating evidences. Some Theosophists, in fact become as dogmatic and absolute in their Theosophical opinions as the most orthodox of Christian fundamentalists. Mme. Blavatsky fully recognized the dangers of such an attitude, foresaw that this might happen, and warned against it in many explicit passages in her work. "*The Secret Doctrine* is not meant to give any such final verdict on existence, but *to lead toward the truth*," she said; [6] and she would be quite unhappy, I am sure, to see how Theossified some of her followers have become. In any case I must reserve the right to doubt Leadbeater's idea of animal "group souls" until provided with some genuine evidence therefor, and I will write the Theosophists a letter of apology if I ever learn that they were right in the matter.

On the other hand their suggestion that the transition from animal to human can be made from several different species is, I think, tremendously provocative, and commends itself to further investigation. It has long been observed that gorillas and chimpanzees are the most similar in form to man and if a Darwinian were to become a reincarnationist he might well believe that the great apes were the ones who first became human. But possibly similarity of bodily structure is not the only consideration. Maybe kinship of faculty is of equal or greater significance. Dogs, for example, have been capable of far nobler and more rational conduct in their relationship to human beings than most apes. Both cats and dogs are similar to man in many temperamental, mental, and emotional traits, and there is an understanding between them and man that, in Occidental countries at least, does not exist between men and monkeys.

It may well be, then, that it is not only one animal that makes the transition from animal to human kingdom.

---

[6] *Mme. Blavatsky on How to Study Theosophy* (Theosophical Publishing House, 68 Great Russell St., London, 1960). See also of *The Key to Theosophy* (Adyar ed., 1933), p. 236.

Maybe several different species cross over simultaneously, and, in doing so, become different types of human beings. One has only to recall how Dr. Samuel Johnson (who disliked the Scots intensely) defined oats in his great English Dictionary—"Oats: a grain which in England is generally given to horses but in Scotland supports the people" —to realize that this notion would lend itself admirably to nationalistic jokes of the future, and could compensate our jokesmiths for the loss of transmigration material.

I must say, though, that the possibility of animals becoming human makes me rather sad, in a way. Animals have perfections and graces all their own and the loss of them in humanization would seem to me rather regrettable. Perhaps this is perverse on my part, but I cannot help thinking with relish of what Mark Twain once said: "If you cross a cat with a human, it will improve the human but deteriorate the cat. . . ." It would make me far happier, I think, to see a dimension somewhere filled with sublimely transcendental felines (whom transcendental humans could visit, sometimes, as a special privilege) than to see all felines transformed into something else. But then I am a notorious felinophile, and you may discount anything I say about cats by ten per cent.

All things considered, we can only conclude, I think, that our questions: Do animals reincarnate? and: Do animals become human beings? stand in need of much research. Theosophical material is in some instances (as with group souls) unbelievable and in some instances provocative, but in all instances unproven. Of Rosicrucian material the same can be said. The Cayce clairvoyance has practically nothing to say on the subject, and we are left really with little more than what we started with—namely, the general notion that if all life is evolving through the cyclic process of reincarnation or re-embodiment, which seems reasonable—then animals, logically, must reincarnate also. How, when, or from what to what, we do not know.

In the midst of all this discouraging vagueness, however, I have been able to come to several certainties with regard to animals. They are certainties for me and I cannot promise that they will become the same for anyone else as they are not mathematically demonstrable.

But for me they are sufficiently compelling to have become the basis for a coherent theoretical outlook and for several practical lines of conduct. Both certainties arise from the work of evidential clairvoyants,[7] and both are confirmed by logic and substantiating fragments of evidence elsewhere. I refer to the clairvoyance of Fred Kimball and that of Edgar Cayce, and I would like to discuss them in that order.

II

The unusual thing about Fred Kimball is not so much the fact that he is clairvoyant. One can find many clairvoyants in the world nowadays. It is the fact that he is clairvoyant with regard to animals.

7 As distinguished from self-styled clairvoyants who often write voluminously descriptive books on their claimed psychic perceptions, yet cannot produce anything of a tangible evidential nature to prove their authenticity.

Kimball is a tall, well-built man who, like many other sensitives, has had little formal education and who has earned his living in a variety of ways. He has been a wrestler, a boxer, and a masseur. Currently (1963) he travels around the world in ships of the merchant marine. The rough seagoing men who are his daily companions seldom guess that this quiet-voiced man leads a double life, and that when he is not acting as steam engineer in the hold of a ship he is pursuing the strange occupation of clairvoyant on land.

Like other clairvoyants, Kimball can see and interpret the aura; perceive significant portions of an individual's past and future; know intimate details about a person's life merely by handling a photograph of him, or a letter; see into the interior of the human body; and make constructive therapeutic suggestions concerning physical and sometimes psychological problems.

Unlike most other clairvoyants, he has taken a special interest in animals. This may be due in part to the fact that he was raised on a New England farm and as a boy knew animals well. In later years, when his psychic gifts first manifested, it occurred to him that he might test his own accuracy of perception by tuning in on the animals at the zoo. He would concentrate on an animal, pick up impressions about it, and question the attendant afterwards to see if the information he picked up corresponded to whatever facts the attendant knew.

I first learned of Kimball through friends of mine in Pasadena who had met him some months before. They invited him to their home one evening, and in the course of their conversation learned of his ability to reach the minds of animals. My friends, who are dog lovers, promptly brought into the room their large Doberman (a dog of the hound variety). Kimball's manner of working is to sit and look at the animal as one looks at a person in conversation. He then begins to ask questions of it aloud. He could just as well ask the questions mentally as orally, but if they are spoken it is easier for the observer to follow what is going on. The animal does not literally "say" or "tell" anything in return; the information is somehow transferred and Kimball merely relays it to the hearer in a conventional manner. I must say that the procedure is a bit startling the first time one witnesses it.

"Do you like the food they give you?" was Kimball's first question to the Doberman. There was a pause. Then he reported: "He tells me that he likes his food except for the fat that you give him."

My friend and his wife exchanged astonished glances. They had had many discussions on this very point. The wife, concerned because the dog's ribs always showed, regardless of how much they fed him, felt they should give him fat in order to plumpen him up. Accordingly they had been giving him suet and the trimmings of fat from chops, roasts, or steaks, and he had been eating them. Kimball could not have possibly known any of this.

"Do you get enough exercise?" was the next question. Another pause as Kimball "listened." Then he said: "He says yes, but he would like to go into the hills more often. You haven't taken him for a while." Again an astonished exchange of glances between husband and wife. Formerly they had taken the dog up into the Pasadena hills almost every week; for the past few months they hadn't had the time for hiking excursions.

"Do you like the beach?" Kimball then asked. The usual pause. Then Kimball said: "He doesn't know what I'm talking about. There's nothing in his mind about beaches." My friends had to admit that they had, in fact, never taken the dog to the beach.

"Do you like the neighborhood?" . . . "He says yes, except that there's a little dog four houses away whose head he'd like to snap off."

My friends were unable to recall any dog for whom the Doberman had shown any marked dislike; in fact, they were unaware of there being any other dog on their street. It was a beautiful residential area, where houses were set far back on spacious landscaped lawns. But some days later when they were walking the dog they passed a house four doors east where a tiny Pomeranian began to yap excitedly from the porch as soon as he saw them. The Doberman continued sniffing at shrubbery and grass, giving the Pomeranian only a disdainful glance from time to time; but now the owners had the feeling that there was, perhaps, an exasperation within him that they had never before surmised.

Some weeks later an animal trainer informed them that it was a great mistake to feed fat trimmings to a Doberman when he lived as confined a life as this one did. Whether or not the dog actually disliked the fat we have no way of proving; nor do we actually know if he had intense feelings of dislike for the Pomeranian. These subjective factors would be verifiable in human beings, but can be known only indirectly, if at all, in animals. But certainly Kimball did pick up certain objective facts about the dog's daily life which, as a total stranger to the neighborhood, the family, and the dog, he had no ordinary way of knowing.

This report intrigued me, and I arranged an evening for Kimball in my own home. I invited sixteen people whom I knew, and eight dogs, none of whom I had ever seen before. It was an exciting evening. Perhaps I should explain that each dog remained in the family car until his turn to be "read"—otherwise things might have been even more exciting than they were.

I think it should be stated at the outset that Kimball, like any other clairvoyant, is not 100 per cent accurate. In the course of the evening he made a number of statements concerning the dogs which the owners could not verify— sometimes because it seemed contrary to what they knew, but more often simply because they did not know. However, in spite of the inevitable margin of error, Kimball's performance that evening was, I felt, quite remarkable.

Skeptics to whom I have spoken about Kimball's faculty, have attributed it to lucky guesses or to "generalizations that would fit any dog." I feel that the things he said, both that evening and other evenings when I have seen him work, were for the most part beyond the reach of lucky guesses, and that, far from being generalities, they were on the contrary quite specific statements regarding unique and sometimes complicated facts in the dog's life. It must be remembered that Fred was a total stranger to everyone in the room, including myself; and I would challenge anyone who thinks his statements to be merely a series of shrewd and lucky guesses to get comparable results on an assortment of eight (or more) strange dogs in another person's living room. Let me cite a few examples.

The first dog to be brought in for a "reading" was a German shepherd dog, part Husky, named Jack. Jack was unused to such a crowd of people, and his excitement was so great that he kept moving about the room from person to person. Kimball kept trying to establish rapport with Jack but finally gave up. "I'm sorry," he said, "but I can't get through to this dog. His mind is too agitated. All that I can get is that he has just about six months more to live." This, of course, the owners could neither affirm nor deny, though they must have in their hearts hoped that Kimball was wrong; and we went on to the next dog without knowing whether Kimball had scored a hit or a miss. The passage of time, however, vindicated him. Just six months later the owners of the dog phoned to tell me that Jack had just died in the veterinarian's hospital.

The next dog to come in was a female German Shepherd by the name of Duchess. Kimball had no difficulty in establishing contact with her, and told the assembled company, after a series of questions to the dog, that she enjoyed riding in the family car, a white station wagon; that she liked to stick her nose out of the window on the left side of the front seat, and that her habit was in fact to rest her head on the driver's neck; that she had a particular attachment to the husband, whom she followed around as much as possible: and that the children seemed to her something of a nuisance. All these details, and others, were confirmed by the owners.

A small mongrel dog, so small in fact that he was sitting on his owner's lap, all bright-eyed attention, "told" Kimball the following things about himself. He lived in a house which was situated just beneath a steep hill. His favorite place to sleep was a leather-covered couch in a room situated next to the bathroom. In the household was a little girl who, whenever she got upset, would go into the bathroom, sit underneath the wash basin, and cry as though her heart would break. The little dog became very unhappy every time this happened. The owner confirmed all the objective description.

Another small dog, a French poodle named Demi Tasse, had quite a different story. "This is a very quiet dog," Kimball said. "Quiet not only in that she doesn't bark much, but quiet in that she doesn't really have very much to say. She doesn't think that anybody is really very much interested in her. She came into your house when she was a puppy and you already had several pets." The mistress nodded. "Yes," she admitted, "we had a cocker spaniel, a white poodle, and a cat." "Well," Kimball continued, "she would have liked to be the only pet in the family. She always had the feeling of being unloved and unimportant. It made her quiet and retiring."

And so the evening went. Some people to whom I have spoken about Kimball's work have dismissed the whole matter easily: Kimball was merely reading the owner's mind. "Merely," they have said, as if to read a man's mind

were no small feat in itself. Actually there is nothing inherently illogical or improbable in the idea that Kimball
should be reading the mind of the animal, except perhaps
to those people who have the deep-seated prejudice that
animals have no minds. But there are in Kimball's work
innumerable instances in which what he relates about the
animals is demonstrably not known to the owner, and yet
can be later substantiated either by investigation, inference, or by putting it to a test. In the case of the Doberman, inference and investigation confirmed at least in part
the validity of what Kimball said. In the case of my cat
Tommy, whom Kimball read at the end of the evening,
I was able to put it to the test.

It was around midnight. The session had come to a close,
and most of the guests were standing around talking. It
was then that my cat Tommy strolled in.

Tommy was a black and white long-haired cat who had
a curiously rakish yet aristocratic look, reminiscent to me
of descriptions of John Barrymore when haughtily drunk.
I happen to live near the Theosophical Society Lodge
building and on warm afternoons and evenings the Theosophists keep the doors of the Lodge open to improve the
ventilation. Tommy had soon learned his way into the
building, where he became as familiar a figure as Matilda
the librarian. Before long he began to sit decorously on the
steps leading to the platform and sometimes even on the
platform itself when lecturers were holding forth. Theosophists may not always be indulgent of such liberties, but
these particular ones were; so Tommy must have listened,

in the several years that he was with me, to dozens of lectures on The Message of Theosophy; The Secret Doctrinc; The Lessons of Atlantis; Personal Memoirs of Madame Blavatsky; and so forth and so on.

He walked into the house this particular evening with his usual aplomb, his black plume of a tail sailing high. Kimball took a careful look at him and then remarked: "That cat has been slowing down lately. I think he has worms and I think there is a green pill that would help him."

My first reaction to this statement was one of disbelief. Tommy was certainly not a sick cat. He had as healthy an appetite as any cat I'd known. I *had* noticed that he was not playing with my other cat, Sunshine, as much as before; but I had not attached any particular significance to this. I merely thought that, what with all those Theosophical lectures, he was growing more serious-minded and studious and let it go at that. So the thought of there being anything physically wrong with him had never once occurred to me; and the thought of worms had certainly never entered my mind.

However, I was sufficiently impressed by what Kimball had done that evening to take Tommy to the animal hospital the following morning, more in the spirit of scientific inquiry than out of any real conviction in the matter. When I phoned in later for a report the veterinarian told me that he had, indeed, been infested with worms. An added detail of interest: in answer to my question, he told me that they did use a green pill for the purpose. And when Tommy returned home—Theosophical lectures or no Theosophical lectures—he *did* begin to be more playful again with Sunshine . . .

III

Now it may well be asked: Why do you attach so much significance to all of this? And I will grant you that the discovery through clairvoyant gifts that a small black and white cat has worms, or that a Doberman dog is yearning to take long walks in the hills, or that a little white poodle named Demi Tasse feels rejected and unloved, does not seem to be of earth-shaking importance, especially on a harassed planet where so many other things are. But it is of significance none the less.

It is significant, first of all, because it demonstrates a new extension in the range of clairvoyance. Clairvoyance has been directed at many targets of interest and undoubtedly other gifted people have looked into the minds and bodies of animals. But seldom, if ever, does one hear of it; and if one does, it is seldom, if ever, accompanied by the evidential details whereby its veracity can be at least partially confirmed.

Kimball's work is deserving, therefore, I feel, of extended study, and what he does should commend itself to other sensitives, for their own exploration. The capacity to enter into the consciousness of animals may prove to be of very great importance to man for the solution of a crime, the finding of lost objects, or the discovery of knowledge concerning the animal kingdom itself.

But Kimball's work has been of interest to me principally because it points, I think, to something of great significance as regards the inner world of animals. Any cat lover or dog lover would find it valuable to know something of what our four-footed friends cannot convey to us through speech. But apart from this immediate and personal satisfaction, there is a broader and deeper implication. Kimball's capacity shows us dramatically that where there is life there is mind and consciousness; that animals are endowed with a sensitive psychological awareness comparable to our own; and that behind their alert bright eyes lies an acute faculty for judgment and appraisal that we ordinarily do not think about because it does not manifest itself in human speech.

Actually this is nothing that has not already been known for a long time; it is only that Kimball's faculty gives the knowledge new immediacy and vividness. Darwin himself stated that the difference in mind between the higher animals and man was one of degree and not of kind. "We have seen," he wrote at the conclusion of several facinating chapters dealing with this question, "that the senses and intuitions, the various emotions and faculties, such as love, memory, attention, curiosity, imitation, reason, etc., of which man boasts, *may be found in an incipient or even sometimes in a well-developed condition in the lower animals.*" [8] (Italics mine.) This observation was based on a large collection of animal incidents and case histories from a variety of sources; and it was later abundantly con-

[8] *The Descent of Man* (Modern Library ed.), pp. 494, 495.

firmed by the systematic laboratory study of animals to which his evolutionary theory gave such impetus.

But man for the most part does not give much serious thought to these similarities between himself and the animal kingdom. If he thinks of them at all, he usually regards them as a curious oddity, rather than as an indication of an intimate linkage in a long chain of life.

This is partly due, no doubt, to native human self-centeredness. It is partly due also to the conditions under which we live. Civilized man dwelling in large cities is profoundly alienated from nature, and has been for many centuries. The average city dweller has little or no contact with the natural life of the animal kingdom; with more and more apartment-house owners enforcing the rule "No Pets Allowed" [9] more and more people are being denied even such minimal contact as a dog or cat allows.

But there is still another factor that has led to our alienation from animals, an ideological one; and it must be frankly acknowledged to be largely the fault of Christian theology. Probably in order to make more emphatic the idea of man's "special creation" early theologians decreed that animals have no souls—a teaching that has no justification in the words of Christ or in the Bible anywhere and for which no scientific proof exists. Even persons who are not aware of the church dogma have the general idea that animals were created only for man's convenience, and if they are Biblically inclined, they will quote you the twenty-

[9] The sign "No pets, children, or musicians" on a Santa Barbara apartment house is some indication of the sterility to which city life is leading us.

sixth line of the first chapter of Genesis, to the effect that man was given "dominion" over "every creeping thing on earth." They forget of course that "dominion" does not mean brutality, tyranny, and cruelty, and they interpret the line narrowly to justify any exploitation they see fit to make.

Unfortunately the gospels included in our present Bible do not explicitly show Jesus as having been concerned about animals, but there are passages in the so-called apocrypha that do. Moreover the One who all his life was compassionate of the lowly and the downtrodden, and who said, "As you do it unto the least of these you do it unto me" could hardly have excluded any sentient life from His compassionate heart or from the intent of His message of love.

In Eastern scriptures there has been a much greater recognition, explicitly stated, of our essential unity with all that lives, and it has not been suppressed to fit the demands of a nature-alienated and egocentric theology. Buddha taught: "One thing only do I teach: suffering and the ceasing of suffering. Kindness to all living creatures is the true religion." Mohammed said to his followers: "There is no beast on earth, nor bird which flieth with its wings, but the same is a people like unto you."

This is precisely the point where Christian ethics, and Western philosophic ethics, are seriously deficient. Both have failed to recognize that an animal is a person; an individual with rights; a being towards whom man has certain obligations. In the last century Schopenhauer was one of the very few philosophers who saw the imperfection of Christian thought and practice in this regard, and the superiority of Buddhist and Brahmin thought and practice. "Look at the revolting ruffianism with which our Christian public treats its animals," he wrote,[10] "killing them for no object at all, and laughing over it; or mutilating and torturing them; even its horses, who form its most direct means of livelihood, are strained to the utmost in their old age, and the last strength worked out of their poor bones until they succumb at last under the whip. One might say with truth, Mankind are the devils of the earth, and the animals the souls they torment."

He pointed out further that in Christian countries we have societies for the prevention of cruelty to animals—to protect them, clearly, from the cruelty of Christians—because in countries where Buddhism and Hinduism prevail, such societies are for the most part unnecessary.[11]

In the present century, Albert Schweitzer has been the most outstanding and the most unforgettable spokesman on this same subject. Pointing out the limitations of our ethical thinkers—Jeremy Bentham, for example, regarded kindness to animals of importance chiefly as practice for kindness to mankind; Kant considered ethics to be concerned only with the duties of man to other men—Schweitzer has affirmed both in his writings and in his entire life

10 "The Christian System," in *The Essays of Schopenhauer* (Wiley Book Co., N.Y.), p. 90.
11 "An extraordinary familiarity exists in India between animals and people of the towns and villages, who treat them as if they were part of the community." *Animals in India,* Ylla (Harper & Bros., N.Y., 1958), p. 90.

work that love must transcend our narrow ethical systems; and that love of and reverence for *all* life must become the pivotal concept of our behavior.[12]

He has reached an awareness that is common to illumined men throughout history. St. Francis regarded all the little creatures as his brothers and sisters. Ramakrishna offended orthodox Brahmin priests by taking offerings of food meant for the Divine Mother and giving them to a hungry cat. The mystical or cosmic consciousness experience almost invariably produces this sense of oneness with all creation. Even LSD experiences frequently result in the same expansion of the boundaries of fellow-feeling. "My many emotions of the day," wrote Jane Dunlap about one of her LSD experiences, ". . . left me with another unshakable conviction . . . : it is that all plants, animals, and humans alike have much the same feelings you and I have. For the first time in my life I became aware of a wonderful oneness existing between all living things, whether plant, animal, or human." [13]

The realization that came to Jane Dunlap through an LSD experience came to me in watching Fred Kimball work. I can no longer look into the eyes of any living creature without feeling that there sits a being of dignity and worth, who looks back into my eyes with grave, sometimes timorous, but always intelligent awareness. I have warned at the outset that the reader may not necessarily be con-

---

12 See *The Animal World of Albert Schweitzer*, ed. by Charles Joy (Beacon Press, Boston, 1950), chapters 14, 15, 16.
13 *Exploring Inner Space*, p. 47.

vinced, merely by reading of my conviction; even if he has the good fortune some day of witnessing Fred Kimball work he may not come to share my conviction.

Yet I do not apologize for my sense of certainty. The certainty is this: Animals are related to us much more closely than we think. Though they lack speech, their mental processes are not very unlike our own. They are similar to us in their fears, their pains, their affections, their frustrations, their terrors, their devotions, their gratitudes, in short, in all their emotions, even though they may know them in lesser complexity and degree than we. They are, as Mohammed said, *a people like ourselves*. Regarded from the evolutionist and reincarnationist point of view, they must be a people struggling along like ourselves, on the long, difficult road to perfection.

It may be aeons before the life wave now animating the animal kingdom will have reached the human level, and at that time we who are now human may have reached another much higher level of development. But regardless of when or how these living beings arrive in our present echelon of consciousness, they are in the truest possible sense of the words *our little brothers,* as Buddha always referred to them and as St. Francis always thought of them.

Each one is to be regarded, then, not as an animated thing, important only as it can serve our own selfish ends, but as a person—a person deserving of as much courtesy and respect as any human being. To the extent that it does not endanger our own survival (for we apparently must still obey that first law of brute survival) we must allow it its own survival. But more than survival, we must, as older brothers, help it in the unfolding of its own potentials, its own intellectual and social faculties, in the same manner as we would help a human child.

A point of view such as this may seem sentimental and downright absurd to most people. But I have come to feel that it is far from absurd, and farther still from sentimental. On the contrary, it is eminently logical and, above all else, supremely practical in terms of our own self-interest.

And this brings me to my second certainty with regard to animals which, as I indicated before, is based upon the work of another clairvoyant, Edgar Cayce.

IV

I think I need not recapitulate here the work of Cayce. Suffice it to say that the whole body of his work points (for those who accept it) to the existence of a moral or ethical law in the universe, which has been called karma.

The case history material in the Cayce files specifically indicates that a human being may generate karma, both positive and negative, with respect to any sphere of nature. People, for example, who are neglectful of land or property in one lifetime are likely to be lacking in land or property in a succeeding life. People who have given much loving care to plants in one life span are likely to be gifted with a green thumb, or with unsuspected wealth accruing from plants, in another incarnation.[14] There are no case histories

---

14 This sort of positive karma was frequently referred to in the Cayce readings—suggesting the possibility that what we call "luck" may be intimately and unexpectedly related to love.

that I recall in the Cayce files wherein a person reaped good or bad karma with regard to the animal kingdom; but the principle would undoubtedly hold true with this as with any other sphere of nature.

On the strength of the whole drift of the Cayce material, then, I believe this proposition can be fairly stated:

A man's attitude toward and treatment of animals is karma-producing, and the karmic reaction good or bad comes to him from the animal kingdom itself.

This is merely a more formalized and specific way of saying: What you do comes back to you. . . . Cast your bread upon the water and you shall find it, after many days. . . .

But sometimes the bread cast on the waters come back very quickly, or, if we wish to use our specialized vocabulary, the karmic reaction is fairly obvious and immediate.

The man who treats his horse kindly and feeds it well is rewarded by a longer lived animal and its greater capacity to pull heavy loads than is the man who treats his horse with neglect and abuse. The farmer who plays music in his barns is rewarded by a richer yield of milk. The old woman, living alone, whose house has caught fire in the night and whose life has been saved by the mewing of her pet cat has been rewarded for her own kindness and hospitality to the cat.

But apart from the material profit which accrues to people who treat animals well—profit arising from the animal itself—there is the more intangible but sometimes more precious benefit arising from the companionship which an animal can afford. "Animals make such wonderful friends," said George Eliot. "They ask no questions, they pass no criticisms." Many a person—disillusioned by the treachery, the perversity, or the stupidity of mankind—has found inexpressible comfort in the company of some little creature. This was true of the French writer Colette. From earliest childhood she had been an animal lover, having come from a family which accepted animals as members of the family. But throughout her life, the disappointments and disillusionments of the love of men led her back again and again to the comforting company of her animals.

Her first husband, Willy, was a writer of sorts who frequently paid other people to do his writing. Discovering that Colette had some interesting schoolgirl memories, and a talent for relating them, he locked her in a room and commanded her to write. Then he published her charming productions under his own name, and amused himself meanwhile with one mistress after another. Except for the literary exploitation, her second marriage followed much the same pattern. "Men were too much for her," her biographer tells us. "She went back to her animals, who seemed to be more reasonable in every way."

Thousands of lonely and heavy-hearted people have discovered this same truth. It is, of course, a pity when people take a disproportionate interest or a neurotic refuge in animals, neglecting their human opportunities or their human obligations. But let us recall that people take disproportionate interest or neurotic refuge in many other things, including religion, scholarship, books, candy, and liquor; and let us recall also that—despite the scorn of those who disparage animal lovers—the percentage of animal lovers who are neurotic is probably no larger than the percentage of neurotic cigarette smokers or neurotic readers of books.

Moreover, there are persons living in isolated places or situations who lack the opportunity of forming human ties. These include the elderly, the blind, and the crippled, childless couples, and single persons who cannot, because of legal restrictions, adopt a child however much they might want to. People such as these and many others can find, and have throughout history found, immeasurable joy in the companionship of a dog, cat, or other creature. The warmth of the relationship—the comfort of a cat who purrs under one's touch, or of the dog who barks joyously on one's arrival—is the karmic reward, truly, of their own affection for and support of the animal. It is a pity that many love-deprived people and many psychologists and social workers dealing with such people do not realize this truth. It is even more the pity that most people who think they "don't like animals" have never stopped to analyze the source of their prejudice, or made the effort to overcome it.

But it is not only things of the heart that come from animals. Much practical knowledge may come from them as well. Animals who are ill stop eating. Man could learn from their instinctive and unspoiled wisdom and go on a fast when he, too, is ill. The Yogis of India acknowledge that they have learned many of their marvelous techniques of health, longevity, concentration, and relaxation through a careful observation of the living habits of animals. Robert Bruce, according to legend, learned perseverance in the face of repeated failure from a spider, whose web was broken again and again yet continued to spin another. The lesson gave Bruce—who was later to be King of Scotland—renewed courage to fight his battle.

That man may learn much from animals, as soon as he alters his attitude of indifference and complacent superiority is, in fact, one of the basic themes of J. Allen Boone's little book, *Kinship with All Life*.[15] Boone had been entrusted with the care of Strongheart, the famous movie dog, during its owner's absence. He had always admired the dog but soon came to respect him for his superlative intelligence, and little by little came to discover that he had much to learn from the dog. The discovery led him on a quest among others who knew and loved animals, and he found that there seemed to be a truth known to them all, even though unknown to the multitudes of men. That truth could be summed up in one word: love. But among its many facets were these commandments: Treat the animal, not as a superior dealing with an inferior, but as an equal. Respect him for the wisdom that is in him. Let him understand that you wish to help him bring out his own best potential. And unfailingly you will not only make a friend, but learn things from him of inestimable importance, whether he be a dog, a skunk, or a rattlesnake. This is the wisdom of all the most successful animal trainers. This was the wisdom of the American Indian and of many other "primitive" peoples. It has been forgotten by "civilized" man and it needs to be learned again.

And so it is not difficult to see the operation of karmic law as regards the treatment of animals in the span of one

15 (Harper & Bros., N.Y., 1954).

lifetime. As you do to them so shall you be done by. There is no reason then why it should seem strange to us when the law operates over a span of many lifetimes.

If a man's life is saved by his pet dog we can easily see the causal connection. But if a man's life be saved by a strange dog, who comes upon him on a lonely road, half pinned under his automobile, and summons a farmer who then brings medical assistance, should we call it "chance"? "Chance is the pseudonym God uses when He does not want to sign His name," wrote Anatole France—which we may interpret in our frame of reference to mean that chance is another name for the Law of God, or karma. Perhaps several centuries ago this man, even though brutish, in a gruff impulse of kindness once extended a helping hand to some little dog in distress. Now he reaps his reward.

Thus many "accidents," either of good or bad fortune, with regard to animals, may be accounted for in terms of good or bad behavior to the animal kingdom before. A child who on a single visit to a farm is crippled or suffers permanent brain damage because of a "chance" kick from a horse may be reasonably assumed to be paying the penalty for his own brutal treatment of a horse or other animal in the past. Or, contrariwise, a person, not ordinarily given to gambling, who wins a great sum of money on a horse race may conceivably be one who has given of himself generously to horses or their welfare in a former existence.

This, then, is the type of reversal, whether of good or bad, which is characteristic of karma. But it becomes clear in the Cayce material that, though karmic action may fre-

quently manifest in this type of reversal, it does not always
do so.

Karma is a psychological principle, having as its purpose
the correction of misevaluations and misconceptions of the
mind which have manifested in conduct. The *change* in the
mind or the psyche is the important thing, and the physical means whereby the educative change is effected is in a
sense secondary and, though always appropriate, subject to
some modifications. And so the karma does not always need
to come from or through the same person, object, or class
of objects that were the recipients of the original harm. I
believe therefore that another proposition may be fairly
stated:

*As a man deals with animals, so shall he be dealt with by
the forces of life in general.*

Consider the case of a woman I know who calls herself a
"teacher of Truth" and believes herself to be "far along
the path of Truth" and "probably on her last incarnation."
Yet she dislikes cats, and has been known to take a stray kit-
ten, which had been befriended by another member of the
household, and deposit it miles away by the side of a busy
highway. Indifferent to its helplessness, without a thought
of the possibility of its being crushed to death, or to linger-
ing agony, by a passing car, or of the even greater tragedy
perhaps of living out a miserable existence, half starved
and at the mercy of sadistic persons, this woman had no
qualms of conscience whatsoever.

She is not much different, except perhaps in her spiritual complacency, from thousands of people who yearly

abandon even their own pet animals in parks or by the roadside on the mistaken assumption that cats and dogs can fend for themselves. Perhaps they can, in a state of nature; but in our present type of city life, where an increasing prevalence of garbage disposal units make it impossible even to find rotting food in garbage pails, abandoned cats and dogs are relatively helpless and come to tragic ends, either by slow starvation, disease, traffic accidents, or deliberate cruelty.

Here then is clearly a violation of the law of love. There is lack of respect for life; there is insensitivity to the suffering of another living creature.

It does not seem likely that the "Truth teacher" and all these other thoughtless and insensitive people should some day be abandoned by a cat or dog, in an exact reversal of situation. But neither does it seem likely that they shall be allowed to continue in their insensitivity. Some educative and probably painful experience will be needed to bring about a change of heart.

Abandoning an animal is cruel enough, but it is a trivial example perhaps by comparison to some of the atrocious cruelties man has inflicted on creatures in his long and brutal history.

Of necessity man has for centuries pressed animals into his service. He has raised sheep for their wool; he has used donkeys, horses, camels, and elephants for transportation; he has made dogs the guardians of his house and cats the guardians of his granary. All of these are in all probability legitimate uses, and if the animal has been recompensed with food, shelter, and protection, it has been in a sense a fair bargain. Every kingdom of nature has a service to give, and the animal kingdom has surely performed its service faithfully and well.

But man has been superior to animals in strength and intelligence, and, like a bully, he has abused his superior position. To this day he often mistreats his dogs and overworks his horses, despite the service they give him. He still stages elaborate, festive, and cruel bull fights, merely for his own amusement. He still hunts and traps even when a real necessity for game or for furs has, for the most part, long since ceased to exist. In slaughterhouses daily he kills animals for food by methods so careless and brutal as not even to be read about without wincing. Most barbaric of all he has persuaded himself that the pursuit of scientific knowledge justifies the excruciating pain of living animals in laboratories where—usually with insufficient if any anaesthetics—he still performs experiments, many of them needless and fruitless because they have been done many times before, that put the tortures of the Inquisition in the class of innocent child's play by comparison.[16]

All such acts, whether of thoughtlessness, neglect, cruelty, or unbalanced and unrestrained science, are the out-

16 "I am without words to express my horror of vivisection, though I have been a teacher of anatomy and surgery for 30 years. It serves no purpose that is not better served in other ways." Prof. James E. Garretson, M.D.

"The law should interfere. There can be no doubt that in this relation there exists a case of cruelty to animals far transcending in its refinement and its horror anything that has been known in the history of nations. . . . There will come a time when the world will look back to modern vivisection in the name of science as we do now to burning at the stake in the name of religion." Prof. Harry J. Bigelow, M.D., Ll.D. Late Professor of Surgery, Harvard University.

ward and visible signs of a lack of sensitivity within, lack of awareness to pain; and it is this grave lack of sensitivity which must be corrected one day, I am convinced, by equivalent agony. The agony, the karma, the man has merited, may in some instances come directly, through animals themselves, in accord with the first proposition above stated. But inasmuch as animals are in a relatively inferior *position* to man (though not of inferior intrinsic worth) the likelihood is that karma may not come through them as often as through other agencies of life, in accord with proposition two. The suffering will of course be appropriate to the nature of the original cruelty.

All men make mistakes in good faith and to all of us come moments of thoughtlessness. A woman, harassed by domestic and financial problems who on one occasion abandons a pet cat in a park, thinking she is doing best by the animal, may not be incurring too much of a karmic debt, if any. The vivisectionist who—sincerely thinking he is contributing to humanity's welfare, and taking careful measures not to cause the animal any unnecessary pain—is surely less guilty than the callous and sadistic man who, with no real scientific justification at all, takes secret pleasure in his power over a helpless cat or dog. But, allowing for single lapses and discounting for well-intentioned if misguided motives, there surely must be a heavy penalty for habitual and repetitive acts of cruelty to animals.

If then a woman has, throughout her lifetime, refused to allow any other members of her household to enjoy the pleasure of a pet animal, the act is sufficiently repetitive to indicate a kind of selfishness and shallowness which needs karmic rectification. I would venture to surmise that in another lifetime, possibly when lonely and old, she will be deprived by apartment-house regulations or by the cruelty of some neighbor of her only companion, some little pet animal. If a man's cruelty has consisted, throughout his adult life, in forcing horses to pull heavy loads, even when they are tired and sick, I would surmise that his own fate, in some other life, may consist in being forced to work by an unfeeling boss or a cruel slave master when in a sick and tired condition. If his cruelty has been that of a pet-shop owner or an animal breeder who has kept many animals in close, uncomfortable confinement, in dirty cages, without light, sunshine, or opportunity for exercise, and with inadequate food, I would surmise that his destiny, on some long distant day, may be to be confined by overseers of a concentration camp, or by the demands of poverty and a crippling illness, in a small, dirty, uncomfortable place, without light, sunshine, or freedom of movement. If his cruelty has been that of a slaughterhouse owner who, knowing full well that painless and certain methods of stunning an animal before slaughter exist, still permits thousands of cattle to be strung up by one hind leg and struck repeated, because often inaccurate, blows on the head with a mallet, then I would venture to guess that one day such callous stolidity will meet with equal brutality, in warfare perhaps or at the hands of criminal bullies. If his cruelty has been that of an experimenter who, in order to "study the effects of shock" [17] has tarred dogs and set fire to them

17 See *Manual of Vivisection,* by Patricia Raymond Dunstan (The Hu-

in a laboratory, or cut them open and poured scalding water into the cavities; or who, in order to make a classroom demonstration of known facts has struck a dog's exposed brain again and again with a steel bar or beaten his hind legs repeatedly with a mallet—he may well be some day the prisoner of a ruthless Nazi-like regime, which has no scruples about performing experiments on living, conscious human beings, or the victim of some cannibalistic tribe which slices off pieces of its victim's body and roasts them in the fire before his living eyes.

I make these equations on a purely speculative basis, I admit, and they may seem disproportionate, even ludicrously so, to the reader, since most people consider animals to be of such paltry significance.

But it must be remembered that what a person does to an animal represents the potential of what he would do to human beings, *provided he had absolute power over them*. A person's conduct toward other human beings is restrained by his own limitations of power. It is often camouflaged by politeness. And it is almost always mixed with some motive of self-interest. But his conduct towards animals is governed by no such restraints. Hence if he is unloving, basically insensitive to the need of another, indifferent, thoughtless, selfish, brutal, cruel—all of these qualities will be seen naked and stripped of disguise in his treatment of any animal that is subject to his will.

---

manitarian League of Rochester, N.Y.), and (Calore Publications, San Pedro, Cal.).

For further information on all humane concerns, write: The Humane Society of the United States, 1145 19th Street N.W., Washington 6, D.C.

If the reader is still unwilling to accept my suggested possible karmic consequences for the mistreatment of animals, let me ask him to imagine himself in the position of a cosmic educator: one whose task it is to take certain souls and place them in a life situation that will bring them out of their immaturity and their insensibility. He may arrive at different corrective situations from those I have proposed, and his proposals may be better than mine. Only clairvoyant or other research can finally establish the truth of the matter. But I would venture to guess that my proposals are true in principle, and that they approximate the particulars at least.

If there is any validity to this line of reasoning, then it would behoove many people to sit back and take serious stock of themselves. It is not enough to say: "I've never abandoned kittens by the roadside, beaten a pet dog, cut off the hooves of a lamb that was still alive, or vivisected a helpless animal!" It is not enough because all about us, in all so-called civilized countries especially including the United States of America, there are thousands of persons who *are* doing these things, daily, without legal regulation or penalty, and *whom we could restrain if only we raised our voices sufficiently loud to achieve some concerted action.* He who permits evil commits evil. If we do *not* raise our voices in the name of decency and humanity we are to some degree guilty, and we have incurred the karmic debt of inactivity, which can of itself be harsh indeed.[18]

---

18 "A person may cause evil to others not only by his actions, but by his inaction, and in either case he is justly accountable to them for the injury." John Stuart Mill.

Women who wear furs of animals who have been trapped with needless cruelty (there are traps in which an animal may lie bleeding, cold, starving, and in the pain of crushed bones for days before the trapper comes to put him to death) are in this delinquent category. All of us who eat meat of animals slaughtered carelessly and with unnecessary brutality, and who make no effort to arouse the conscience of legislators or slaughterhouse owners, share inescapably in the guilt. So long as we allow private medical interests and medical schools the right of pound seizure—which means the right to seize uncalled for or lost pets in city animal shelters and use them for research—and the right of unsupervised experimentation on animals (often, by their own admission, stolen from city streets) without investigating the infamous conditions and sadistic practices with which most of this research is done—research moreover which is both unnecessary and fruitless in the opinion of many medical men themselves—we are participators in the outrage. "No one may shut his eyes," said Albert Schweizter, "and think that the pain which is therefore not visible to him is nonexistent." [19]

All of this may be regarded as sentimental concern only so long as we are far removed, in our comfortable and smartly decorated apartments, from the horrible sights and sounds of animal slaughter and animal experimentation, and only so long as we can still maintain the theoretical position that animals are merely *things,* created for man's use and abuse. But once it is seen that all life is interrelated; that all life is traveling together on the same long

[19] *The Animal World of Albert Schweitzer,* p. 191.

and difficult pilgrimage; that between man and animal there are ancient and complicated bonds of relationship; that every act has its consequences to the performer of the act; that the universe operates on a strict and inescapable ethical foundation—then it must be seen that to treat any animal with anything but the same consideration that we would wish accorded to ourselves is short-sighted folly of the most imbecilic kind.

For animals are not only souls evolving in their own right; souls who need help and guidance in their evolvement as we need help and guidance in ours; souls who need our friendship, interest, and compassionate assistance in the many tragic and difficult vicissitudes of their life. *They are also the symbolic representation of any unit of life which is relatively helpless in comparison to our own strength, and any intelligence which is relatively inferior to our own.*

Thus they become the materials upon which all of our own tendencies are exercised, the tests upon which the Power and Superiority aspects of our own souls are given searching examination. The tests which they provide are comparable in every way to those which other human beings provide; and these test situations become the matrix in which karmic consequences on every level of being originate.

At the same time animals represent an index—not an infallible index to be sure, but nonetheless a deeply significant one—to the degree of spiritual evolvement of the people who stand in relationship to them. In psychiatric interviews questions such as: "How do you feel about your father?" "How do you feel about your mother?" "How do you feel about sex?" are commonly asked. A question of just as crucial diagnostic signifiance would be: "How do you feel about animals?"

The conscience of mankind is gradually awakening. Step by step it grew to the point where it recognized that slavery was an evil; that the exploitation of children was an evil; and that the suppression of women was unenlightened. We are now in a stage of history where the exploitation of one country by another, and one people by another, is also being recognized as improper. This change in political philosophy is accompanied by tumultuous upheavals all over the world. The simultaneous awakening of the conscience of mankind as regards animals might seem inconsequential, by comparison with such global changes and tumults; yet it is intimately related and complementary to them. For it is part of the growing realization, if still dim and confused, that *all life is one.*

I can envision a more enlightened civilization than our own in which poverty, unemployment, and war will have ceased, and disease and crime will be greatly abated. In that saner and happier world there will be a sense of interrelatedness among the human beings of this planet, and possibly even between the inhabitants of our planet and those of other worlds in space. But certainly in such a world there will be a sense of fellowship between mankind and all the beautiful creatures who are his younger brothers in the great pilgrimage of life.

In such a world I can envision certain salient features of man's relationship to animals.

1) All schools will have courses in ethics—an ethics unrelated, perhaps, to any religious system, but based on the pivotal and nonsectarian concept of reverence for life. In such courses the right treatment of animals (as well as of humans) and the interdependent, interrelated nature of all the kingdoms of life will be taught.

2) All children will be allowed a pet animal by their parents, and trained for participation in society by being taught from the beginning the considerate and responsible treatment of their pet.

3) Mistreatment, neglect, and willful abandonment of an animal will be regarded as an offense punishable by law. Cruelty will be considered indicative of the need for psychiatric treatment.

4) Remarks like "I hate cats" or "I don't like animals" will be regarded as symptomatic of some kind of immaturity, or of a phobia brought over from a past life which needs psychological treatment.

5) If humanity continues to eat meat, the transportation and slaughter of animals will be done under conditions outlawing terror and cruelty.

6) Vivisection will be outlawed, it being found possible to obtain biological knowledge by other methods, and it being recognized that no end justifies an evil means.

7) Bull fights, fox hunts (which Oscar Wilde called the pursuit of the uneatable by the unspeakable) and other cruel sports will be outlawed.

8) Animals may still be used in the service of man, but

the treatment of them will always be kind and considerate. The training of animals will be regarded as useful to the animal in its ongoing evolution as it is to the human being.

9) Most families will have not only one pet, but two pets of the same or different species, that they may have the security and pleasure of each other's company.

10) Institutions such as old people's homes, children's hospitals, orphanages (if such institutions still exist as we know them), possibly even prisons, will allow inmates to have pet animals for companionship and as part of their rehabilitative program.

11) Apartment-house owners and landlords may require a refundable deposit against any possible damage to property done by a pet animal, and may establish other regulations regarding animal behavior in order to keep harmony among tenants; but the "No Pets Allowed" ruling will be regarded with great social disfavor.

These may seem exaggerated and impractical notions to some and—taken out of context—would lend themselves beautifully to an S. J. Perelman type of ridicule. But they will not seem ridiculous when man truly regards the oneness of life as a fact and not as a visionary notion, and animals are recognized for the younger brothers that they are.

In the meanwhile, we live in an age of barbarism. We would do well, all of us who have begun to think seriously about these matters, to recall a prayer first uttered by St. Basil, Bishop of Caesarea, in A.D. 370:

O God, enlarge within us the sense of fellowship with all living things, our little brothers to whom Thou hast given this earth as their home in common with us.

May we realize that they live not for us alone, but for themselves and for Thee, and that they love the sweetness of life even as we, and serve Thee better in their place than we in ours.

8

TWO CORRECTIVES FOR THE
CONFUSIONS OF OUR TIMES
Reincarnation and General Semantics

George Bernard Shaw once remarked that this planet was probably the lunatic asylum of the solar system.

Personally, I have been more inclined to be charitable in the matter and merely call our planet the kindergarten of the system; but on the other hand there are days (of increasing frequency lately) when I think George Bernard Shaw may have been right.

When I was a student at the University of Wisconsin I remember reading an anecdote concerning the mental institution that was situated just across the lake from the campus. It seems that a visitor from Milwaukee was looking for the university, but having taken the wrong turn of the road, he found himself in front of a group of buildings that somehow looked unlike a college campus. "Isn't this the university?" he asked a man standing at the gate. No, the man informed him, this was the state lunatic asylum. "Well," quipped the traveler. "I guess there isn't too much difference between the two institutions." "Oh, yes there is," returned the attendant with dignity. "You have to show improvement to get out of here."

It was a significant statement, I thought at the time. And

it seems to me to be still significant. Whether lunatic or not, the residents of this planet are going to have to show a lot of improvement to get out of the mess we are all in; and unless the improvement is rapid, cataclysmic disaster may overcome us all.

There are many people nowadays who believe they know a way to save the world. Usually their plan of salvation is through some kind of social, political, or religious reform. I am thoroughly in favor of reform in all three of these areas; but I am profoundly dubious that any of these approaches, singly or together, holds the total answer to our planetary dilemmas. A mere change of condition, when superimposed on people who do not themselves have new insight, can only revert to the same evils and abuses that characterized the old condition.

So I am convinced that for any proposed reforms to be truly effective and lasting there needs to be a new kind of insight in human beings, insight of a psychological, scientific, and philosophic nature. I would like therefore to raise my voice in favor of the widespread and immediate dissemination of knowledge concerning two things: the theory of reincarnation and the methodology of General Semantics.

The mention of two such vastly different approaches in the same breath may seem somewhat surprising to some people. To most General Semanticists I know, it would be more than surprising; it would be horrifying. General Semanticists, in the main, are not very kindly disposed toward such matters as reincarnation or even parapsychology. And so at best they would consider my two solutions as very strange bedfellows. At worst, they would regard them, angrily, as highly improper bedfellows, much as white southerners would regard the idea of Negroes marrying their sisters.

I admit that the juxtaposition of two such widely differing systems of thought *is* somewhat odd, at least at first glance. The theory of reincarnation and the methodology of General Semantics originate from diametrically opposite presuppositions—the former from religious and philosophic traditions, and the latter from logical positivism, empiricism, and twentieth-century philosophy of science. And yet curiously enough there is a meeting ground between them. When both approaches are fully—not superficially known—it can be seen that many of their differences are complementary, that each enriches the other in surprising new ways, and that both can contribute immeasurably to the sanity of the inhabitants of our planet.

This is true even though we consider reincarnation only as a theory, and General Semantics only as a pragmatic method.[1] I must admit at the outset that 1) an unproven theory of itself could hardly be remedy for anything, and 2) it seems illogical to link a theory about the universe with a methodology of speech, behavior, and evaluation.

However, with regard to the first point, it must be recognized that there are theories that are ill-founded and

[1] General Semantics is also, basically, a theory of sanity and of meaning, and it involves certain theoretical considerations which have been sharply challenged by some critics. But oddly enough, even many of those who criticize its theory acknowledge the efficacy of its methods, as for example the Catholic scholar and educator, Mother Gorman. See: *The Educational Implications of the Theory of Meaning and Symbolism of General Semantics,* by Mother Margaret Gorman, R.S.C.J., Ph.D. (Catholic University of America Press, Washington, D.C., 1958).

those that are well-founded; and I would not regard the reincarnation theory as a possible corrective of the world's confusions if I did not feel it to be a well-founded one. It is an axiom of science that, in the absence of evidence which is conclusive, that theory is best which most completely and successfully accounts for and correlates the greatest number of unexplained phenomena. Reincarnation meets this criterion.

It may not commend itself to all people, of course. But to those who have sufficient intellectual curiosity to examine it in all its logical, inferential, and evidential aspects, it more often than not results in a sense of inner conviction. This conviction then in turn results in some extraordinarily healthful consequences, mental, moral, and emotional. The theory, then, has important practical results in the daily conduct of life; and this is why, with respect to the second point noted above, it is not so illogical to link it with the discipline of General Semantics as it might at first glance appear.

Several basic features of the reincarnation theory are responsible for its practical usefulness. It deals, for one thing, with order, structure, and relations within the universe. It postulates an orderly universe which is purposive; it affirms that there is a structural pattern underlying the seeming chaos of life, a pattern based on the cyclic reappearance of all life units, under a law of equilibrium called Karma; it places human beings in interdependent and unitary relationship with each other and with all other kingdoms of life.

A point of view such as this differs drastically from

widely prevalent outlooks in the world today. Thousands of people in both hemispheres have lost faith in the traditional religious systems. Some of them, feeling the need of a nonmaterial set of values, have turned to the philosophy of Humanism, or to revolutionary programs of social reform. These approaches have nothing to say about an afterlife; but they have become substitutes for religion in that they give purpose to life beyond self-interest, and they have concern for the welfare of other human beings.

But thousands of other people have found no such philosophy and no such program of action; and they live lives governed almost entirely by self-interest and expedience, restrained by no moral code, sweetened by very little concern for other human beings, and undirected by any sense of cosmic meaning. A materialistic style of life such as this is highly vulnerable, however, in a world as uncertain as ours has always been and as perilous as it now peculiarly is. Purely materialistic goals are subject to frustrations on every hand; and frustration may lead to aggression and hostility on the one hand, or to the sense of futility and hopelessness on the other. It is no wonder then that juvenile delinquency, alcoholism, drug addiction, suicide, violence, promiscuity, and crime are rampant.

The reincarnation theory, however, with its affirmation of an orderly and purposive universe, leads almost inevitably, in people who accept it, to behavior which is more orderly and purposive, more filled with hope and affirmativeness. The concept of karma becomes a deterrent to evil acts in the manner that hell used to be a deterrent in an age more naïve than our own; but karma has, in a scientific age, more force than hell because it is seen to be a scientific principle, and hence unfailing in action and not subject to special pleading or special favors on the part of paid and possibly venal prelates.

For who would continue to act barbarically to people of another race when he knows that, as an inevitable karmic consequence, he will himself some day be the member of a race that is barbarically treated?

Who would persist in unethical business practices, in duplicity and double dealing, knowing that the bookkeeping of the universe is unfailing, and he will himself become the victim of exactly that which he has done to others?

Who would continue to mistreat a helpless creature, animal or human, when he knows that he is thereby decreeing his own future fate?

Who would continue to ignore the plight of the destitute, the hungry, the dispossessed, knowing that this very indifference must be made into concern by the experience of equal or comparable sufferings?

In short, the exhortations "Love one another" and "Do unto others as you would have others do unto you" become, by this perspective, commandments that have as their foundation, not merely religious idealism, but laws of physics and mathematics that cannot be circumvented. The cultivation of love and brotherly behavior is seen then not to be a mere form of effeminate sentimentality, but a practice which is soundly founded in law and rigor of a strictly masculine kind.

For all these reasons, and many more, the theory of reincarnation, widely disseminated at this derelict time in the world's history, can be of immeasurable transforming power. It can restrain those who would otherwise do purposive or aimless evil; it can act as a powerful stimulus to good among those whose wills now have no compass and no direction. It can release people from the terror of death and of atomic destruction; it can reassure them that their suffering is meaningful, and that their lives, however obscure, are greatly significant.

Turning from reincarnation to General Semantics, we find ourselves in quite a different climate of thought. General Semantics has been in existence since 1933, but it is still a relatively unknown subject and a good many misunderstandings about it exist in the mind of the general public.

It seems scarcely credible, but it is true, that some people confuse it with ceramics. Other people say, Oh, yes, they would love to take a course in it, as they have always wanted to increase their vocabulary. And still others, a little more sophisticated, say that the study of words and the history of word changes has always fascinated them. These people are, of course, thinking about semantics. This latter confusion is perhaps the most widespread, and the most unfortunate. There is a vast difference between semantics and General Semantics.

Semantics does, to be sure, deal with words; and so, in a way, does General Semantics. However General Semantics is concerned not only with words but also (as one person put it) with what words do to people and what people do to words. It is deeply preoccupied with a matter that in large part has been ignored by academic psychology, namely, the pervasive and often pernicious effect of language on human mental and emotional life. However General Semantics—or G. S., as it is widely called—is basically interested also in the inadequacy of words to capture and express reality. It deals as much with reality, the knowing process, and our errors of perception and inference as it does with the words with which we convey our often erroneous perceptions and inferences to each other.

G. S. might therefore be defined as a new technique of thinking; but it must be carefully distinguished from another contemporary technique known as New Thought or Positive Thinking. Positive Thinking for the most part is based on various religious presuppositions about God and man's relationship to God. G. S., on the contrary, has no religious presuppositions whatsoever and bases itself entirely on various insights of twentieth-century linguistics, anthropology, physics, and mathematics. It is, as Alfred Korzybski, its originator, rather formidably put it: "the epistemological non-Aristotelian methodology of thought." But it is also, as one writer has stated, "the science of how not to be a damn fool."

And this, though it may seem flippant, is truly an excellent definition; for this new scientific way of thinking inevitably flows into a new, saner, and more rational way of behaving, and into a less befogged and delusional way of talking; and thus much damn-foolishness is either avoided completely or greatly minimized.

Unfortunately the full force of any of these definitions, and all others I might give, is appreciable only after one has actually applied the discipline for a period of some time.

The basic book of this new approach was written by Alfred Korzybski, a Polish engineer and mathematician. It is called *Science and Sanity* and I recommend, strongly, that you do not read it. Not unless, that is, you have a mathematical- or engineering-type brain and not unless you are prepared to work your way through about 800 pages of a diffuse and rather badly organized book. G. S. is far better approached by the average person through one of its many popularizations.[2]

None the less, *Science and Sanity* (rather like Blavatsky's *The Secret Doctrine,* in a way, which is also long, badly written, and diffuse) remains a monumental contribution to human thought and will reward any student who has the patience to study it.[3] It was published in 1933 and since that time its insights and techniques have little by little seeped down to all strata of society.

This is one of the many surprising things about G. S.: it is usable by people of all ages and in practically every field of human endeavor. It has been taught to six-year-olds with notably good effect. In Santa Monica, California, it is being successfully taught to children in the fourth grade as well

[2] Such as, for example: *How To Develop Your Thinking Ability,* Kenneth Keyes (McGraw Hill Book Co., N.Y., 1950); *Language Habits in Human Affairs,* Irving Lee (Harper & Bros., N.Y., 1941); *Communication: Patterns and Incidents,* William Haney (Richard D. Irwin, Inc., Homewood, Ill., 1960).

[3] *Science and Sanity: An Introduction to Non-Aristotelian Systems and General Semantics,* by Alfred Korzybski (International Non-Aristotelian Library Publishing Company; distributed by Institute of General Semantics, Lakeville, Conn.).

as to children in junior high school. In scattered places all over the country, high school and college students are learning it. Yet adult specialists in almost any field you might mention find it a useful and highly potent adjunct to whatever they already know.

Teachers, for example, find that it improves classroom discipline, removes many sources of teacher-student antagonism, and tends to integrate in a student's mind the "subjects" of his curriculum which ordinarily remain unrelated lumps. Psychologists find that it is usable in a wide range of neurotic disorders, including homosexuality, frigidity, impotence, phobias of all kinds, and alcoholism; they also find that it tends to shorten substantially the period of treatment. Businessmen have found that G. S. improves the communication process between management and personnel, as well as between the organization itself and the general public. In Chicago, police officers have been trained with G. S. methods, with resulting better efficiency on their job in meeting the public. At San Quentin prison classes in the subject are attended voluntarily by many inmates, a number of whom testify to the fact that it is the only thing that to them has made any sense. One highly intelligent prisoner wrote, after his release, to the instructor: "After many years of Christianity, and four years of Alcoholics Anonymous, I must say that my six months of General Semantics did more for me personally and intellectually than anything I had ever been exposed to. It is the only thing of any real rehabilitative merit that I know about. I feel it should be taught in every prison in the country." So wide a scope may seem exaggerated and, indeed, almost

incredible, until one has experienced the method for oneself.

The foregoing may serve, then, as a general introduction
to the subject. The manner in which it actually operates
can at least in part be seen by taking under consideration a
problem which has always confronted mankind, namely
the relationship of man to man. This problem has always
been with us; but for many reasons well known to everyone, it is of more crucial importance now than ever before.

All the great religious teachers of whom we have any
record have been concerned with this problem. Jesus said
"Love one another"; "Love your neighbor as yourself";
"Do unto others as you would have others do unto you."
Buddha and Maimonides, Mohammed and Confucius,
Baha-u-lla and indeed all of the Wise Ones of the world
have phrased it in their own manner, but have said substantially the same thing. The ideal of brotherhood has
been widely taught throughout the centuries and undoubtedly these exhortations have had some ennobling effect on
mankind. Unfortunately they have not been practiced as
much as they should have been, and, in fact, we might well
make a simple diagnosis of the world's present misery and
confusion and say that it is due to the lack of brotherly love.

Brotherly love, to be sure, is probably something that
cannot be taught. But brotherly behavior *can* be taught—
especially when its close relationship to enlightened self-
interest and improved general efficiency is made clear. We
have already seen how the reincarnation theory, with its
correlative principle of karma, tends to promote brotherly

behavior. We shall now approach the same problem from the perspective of a General Semanticist.

The General Semanticist, to be sure, might not want to use the words "brotherhood" or "brotherly love," as he would tend to regard the terms as "high order abstractions." This astringent attitude might alienate some people at first; but, with patience, they would find out that beneath the General Semanticist's stern armor of vocabulary there beats a heart of gold, so to speak, and that while he would prefer to talk in terms of time-binding, survival, and communication, he is none the less as much and as terribly concerned about the lack of brotherhood and the plight of the human race as is anybody else.

Communication is, in fact, a key word and a key concept in the General Semantics system. Perhaps we can best approach an understanding of this concept by considering a cartoon published some years ago in the *Saturday Evening Post*.

The cartoon shows two farmhouses, some distance apart, which have been snowed in and isolated after a heavy snowstorm. The man of each house has begun to dig a path to the house of his neighbor. Each has dug a pathway about two thirds of the distance between two houses. They have missed each other by about eight feet and neither knows of the other's efforts. There is no caption under the cartoon, but it needs none. The scene itself is a mute ironic commentary on the tragedy of men when they are not in communication. Wasted time, wasted energy, and needless duplication of effort were the consequences; and when the two men finally discovered what had happened there must also have been feelings of annoyance, frustration, and even anger.

From the point of view of General Semantics much of human misery and confusion is due to just such a lack of, or breakdown of, communication among people who actually may have no lack of brotherly intent; they merely have gotten bogged down and deflected and confused by the limitations of language, or their own failure to use it properly.

Here is a simple example from daily life. One rainy day after school a young practice teacher—filled with ideals and love of children and love of humanity, no doubt—was trying to put on little Johnny's raincoat and galoshes. The raincoat slipped on easily enough but the galoshes were too tight, and she struggled and shoved and pushed and tugged until finally she managed to force them on. "These overshoes seem a little tight," she said brightly to little Johnny. "That's 'cause they're not my overshoes," he piped, sweetly. Aghast, the young teacher struggled and shoved and pushed and tugged until finally she got them off again. "They're my brother's," little Johnny explained, when the operation was complete. "I just wear them 'cause I haven't got any of my own."

It can be imagined that the young teacher's feelings of brotherly love were sorely tested at this point, if not completely shattered for the rest of the day.

What was the mechanism of the situation? A childlike failure on the part of little Johnny to communicate necessary information. This was a trivial incident, of minor importance; but human life is made up of trivialities and a long succession of minor annoyances can destroy the most beautiful relationship, or wear away the most dedicated idealism.

Domestic squabbles are often caused by failures of communication of this very type. A husband, for example, fails to notify his wife that he will be late for dinner. Only three minutes of time and ten cents of the coin of the realm would have prevented the worry, the anxiety, the impatience, the anger, and finally the fury of a woman whose dinner is ready and who does not know where her husband is or why. Affectionate consideration should, of course, be the mainspring of action in a husband in such situations; but even prosaic and undemonstrative husbands, who have long since lost whatever sentiment or consideration they may once have had, can see the engineering logic of the necessity for an open communication line, if maximum efficiency of service is to be maintained. Many a divorce could have been avoided had there been a sensitivity on the part of both husband and wife merely to the need for open communication lines.

History and literature are filled with tragedies of great magnitude that happened basically not because of an accumulation of small communication failures, but because of one small but crucial communication failure.

Consider, for example, De Maupassant's famous little classic, "The Necklace."

This is the story of Mathilde, a pretty young woman who was invited with her husband to a ball. The husband was a humble little clerk at the Ministry of Public Instruction and could barely manage to buy her a new gown for the occasion. Mathilde decided to ask a former schoolmate, who was very rich, if she might borrow a piece of jewelry. The friend willingly let her choose whatever she wished; Mathilde selected a beautiful diamond necklace and wore it triumphantly to the party, where she had an exhilarating evening. On arriving home, however, she discovered that somehow she had lost the necklace. Frantically the husband retraced all their steps, but to no avail. He made her write a note to the friend, saying that they were having a broken clasp repaired; in the meanwhile they intensified their search. The necklace was not to be found. Hunting through all the jewelry shops they finally found a necklace which closely resembled the one they had lost. It cost 34,000 francs—money which they did not have and which they borrowed from every possible source at frightful rates of interest.

Mathilde brought the replica to her friend, who received it coldly, saying, "I might have needed it before this." Then began a life of privation and drudgery. The husband had to take on extra work at night. To economize they took a cheaper dwelling, in a garret, and dismissed their peasant serving woman. Mathilde drudged and toiled at all sorts of heavy housework. It took them ten years to pay off their mountainous debts. Then one day Mathilde saw her old friend on the street. The friend did not recognize Mathilde—she had changed so much. On a sudden impulse Mathilde told her what had happened years ago. "Oh, my poor Mathilde!" said her friend. "Why, my necklace was paste! It was not worth five hundred francs."

A certain literary critic, in analyzing this story, said that the key to the tragedy was the daydreaming, the vanity, and the pride of Mathilde. There is certainly truth in this analysis. But it is equally true to say that a key to this tragedy lay in a failure of communication. If Mathilde had spoken frankly and promptly to her friend about what had happened, she would have learned the truth about the value of the necklace and two lives would have been spared ten years of ruinous frustration, anxiety, and toil. Mathilde and her husband were *assuming* something about the necklace, namely, that it was what it appeared to be. An opened communication line would have shown in a few minutes the mistaken nature of their assumption. Frustration, which as we know leads more often than not to hostility and aggression, need not have been theirs. How much brotherly love did Mathilde and her husband have the strength or the spirit to manifest in those ten gruelling years, and after?

The foregoing examples have been instances where there has been no attempt at communication. But there are as many, or more, instances in human life where the effort has been made to communicate, but somehow the communication breaks down.

These, too, range from the trivial to the tragic; but in all cases they threaten that amicable feeling between people that is essential if brotherhood is to prevail.

Breakdowns in communication often result from the fact that in the English language, as in every language that we know of on this planet, we have a limited number of words to express an infinite number of things. Many words in our language have two or more dictionary meanings (such as *just, fair, board*) and many others (such as *run, fix, fast*) have a whole constellation of meanings, some related and some unrelated to the same basic idea. Still others— like *sail* and *sale, sight* and *site, prey* and *pray*—are different in spelling but have the same sound and can easily be confused in conversation. To assume, therefore, that you have understood exactly what someone else has said, and *to act immediately on this assumption,* may be very dangerous and very costly.

A beautiful example of this kind of confusion, again from the world of childhood, is seen in the case of the boy who came home tearfully from school, telling his mother that the teacher had said she was going to drop him into the furnace. Furious, the mother marched to school the next morning and confronted the principal with this dreadful threat on the part of the teacher. Considerably agitated himself because of the mother's agitation, the principal proceeded to the teacher's room to face her with the accusation. The teacher had no idea what they were talking about, until she remembered that the previous day she had said: "Robert, if you don't behave yourself I will drop you from the register."

Register, to little Robert, meant only one thing: the grating on the floor that led down to the furnace. Four and maybe five emotionally disturbed people: the child, the mother, possibly the father, the principal, and the teacher —*all because one word was misunderstood.* In all this whirlpool of agitation the tenuous threads of brotherly love were surely strained and torn.

Had this mother been a student of General Semantics, she would have known something of the pitfalls of language and the whole communication process. She would therefore have taken a tentative attitude rather than a fixated one, a questioning approach rather than a belligerent one. She would have asked a question: *Are you sure you understood the teacher correctly?* before jumping to an angry conclusion.

Let us consider now a rather expensive example from the realm of business—an incident which happened to a Chicago merchandising manager of a firm making television sets.[4] He had ordered a slide film from a visual aids firm in order to explain his new television model to his distributors. A few weeks before the meeting of distributors was to take place he decided to change one frame of the film. He phoned the visual aids technician and said: "I want a picture of a stationary core with three or four small dots circling around it. Do you get what I mean?"

"Sure," the technician replied. "I can't promise delivery till the day before your meeting, though."

The film was duly delivered, and the merchandising manager was horrified when he saw what the technician had done. He had shown four dots moving in independent circles, each in a corner of the frame; whereas what the manager had wanted was three or four dots moving around the central core in concentric circles, in the manner of planets revolving around a sun. Since two hundred copies of the film had been made for the dealers to take back to

4 "How To Say What You Mean," *Nation's Business* (May, 1957).

their salesmen, the cost of correcting this little misunderstanding came to exactly two thousand five hundred dollars. . . .

From the article in which the case was reported we do not know much about the manager's reaction to the incident; but it is quite possible that he behaved as businessmen in authority often do behave under such circumstances, namely, with explosive anger, profanity, and a slamming down of the telephone, followed by ill-humored irritability for the rest of the day towards his secretary, his subordinates, his wife, his children, and the family cat —surely a strain on the brotherly love of everybody within reach.

Moral exhortations such as "Love one another," "Love suffereth long and is kind," or "Be not wrathful with fools" are beautiful sentiments and ennoble the mind as one reads them, no doubt; but in emergencies of this type they often fail of cogency. A scientific insight into the basic cause of this little disaster, however, namely, a communication failure, is much more healing to the nerves and much more likely to prevent a recurrence of similar disasters in the future. This scientific insight is one of the things that General Semantics provides.

The words "three or four dots revolving around a central core" do not have different dictionary meanings; but they are susceptible of many varying interpretations. You may yourself find half a dozen ways of interpreting the phrase "revolving around," or an infinite number, really, since an infinite number of planes can be drawn through a single point and hence dots "revolving around" the point could be shown in any one of those planes.

The directions, in short, were ambiguous. Maybe some day telepathy will be a universal faculty, but until such time nobody has the right to expect that anybody else can read his mind. Consequently, whenever we give another person verbal directions—especially when these concern matters of great importance—we must make certain that he has really understood what we have said. We can draw a diagram, as the merchandising manager should have done for the visual aids technician. We can define our terms with precision; we can ask the other person to repeat what we have said to make sure he has grasped our intent; we can suggest that he ask us questions concerning whatever is not clear. If these precautions are taken, we have better chances of a successful communication, and a major source of irritability, frustration, anger, and waste among human beings is done away with.[5]

It would certainly be an oversimplification to suggest that all human problems are due to linguistic failures of this type. In fact, some critics take issue with the G. S. literature in that it seems to make just such an oversimplification. Their point is well taken; I myself have at times deplored the seeming tendency in some General Semantics writers to exaggerate linguistic factors and ignore factors

[5] For an excellent treatment of this problem and how to deal with it, see *Handling Barriers in Communication*, by Irving Lee and Laura Lee (Harper & Bros., N.Y., 1956). This handbook is the text of a course given to employees of the Illinois Bell Telephone System.

of character. Selfishness, malice, greed, envy, and lust are realities of the human world (even if General Semanticists *do* call the words "high order abstractions") and they will wreak havoc in human relations no matter how well communication lines are kept open and no matter how careful and intelligent our use of language. But, on the other hand, General Semanticists have called attention to a much neglected and immensely important matter, and perhaps one third of human misery could be alleviated or prevented completely if communication failures were eliminated.

Thus far we have discussed certain aspects of the problem of the relationship of man to man. Right relationships in this sphere would greatly improve the condition of the world, and both reincarnation and G. S. can help contribute to that end.

But there is another terrible source of confusion today, and this is in the realm of the right relationship of man to the reality of the universe.

There is a strange discrepancy prevalent between the scientific knowledge that exists and that makes revolutionary changes in the physical world possible, and what the average man knows about such knowledge. The insight of atomic physicists, for example, has transformed the entire aspect of warfare and of the world; but the same insight is not generally integrated into the workday knowledge of the average citizen.

More specifically, the physicist knows that what we call matter is illusory. Matter is a certain configuration of energies. It appears solid but it is not. It appears to be at rest but in reality it is a dynamic process or an event. To our senses a table is a table. At a deeper level of reality the table is an event that is happening.

The physicist deals far more with invisible forces and realities than he does with visible ones. He uses sound waves beyond the range of human hearing to cut steel or to clean the lamps of a great city; he deals with atomic particles that are completely beyond the range of human sight to generate unthinkable power. The physicist knows that the philosophy of materialism is untrue and untenable. Materialism is dead, but millions of persons seem never to have been notified of the funeral.

This number includes, unfortunately, the majority of psychologists, psychiatrists, logicians, theologians, doctors, politicians, and teachers, who have not yet recognized the vast implications of this revolution in thinking for their own profession. As a race, therefore, we must present a curious spectacle, which might be symbolized by these analogies. We are like a man wearing a toga and sandals, riding in the elevator of a 60-story building. We are like a lady wearing a hoop skirt and a powdered wig, sitting at the wheel of a 1963 Cadillac. We are like a man wearing a leopard skin loincloth, sitting at the controls in a hydrogen-bomb-carrying plane. . . . We are, in short, a race of people who has not yet caught up with its own technology.

Both the theory of reincarnation and the methods of General Semantics, however, are in harmony with the insights of modern physics; and more than merely being in harmony with it, they suggest profound changes in attitude and behavior which are in accord with it. Thus both serve to heal the schism in our psyche and both serve to bring man into harmony with the actual world in which he is living.

The reincarnation theory does this because by its very nature it emphasizes the reality of many invisible things, but not irresponsibly, in the manner of a hallucinating mental patient, nor superstitiously, in the manner of a theology that has confused metaphors for fact and poetry for prose. It does so responsibly and coherently, with certain important evidential points of agreement with known and knowable facts of psychology and of physics.

The being which resides in the body is invisble. The laws and the forces of karma are invisible. The vast patterns of relationship and interrelationship over long arcs of time are, to mortal sight, invisible. But they are not the less real for their invisibility. The Ancient Wisdom of which reincarnation is an essential part has also long taught the reality of other invisible matters, such as the primacy of thought and the power of thought to control matter—realities which parapsychology is only now beginning to substantiate in laboratories; yet they were described in great detail in Mme. Blavatsky's book in 1888, as were also many of the major discoveries of modern physics.

General Semantics did not precede modern physics, as did the reincarnation theory; originating in 1933, it consciously incorporated, rather, the new insights into its system. It is, in fact, the only organized method of logic, evaluation, and therapy in our times that does. Fully to explain this statement would involve an explanation of the entire system; but one aspect of it at least can be indicated here.

Korzybski made an interesting and useful device called

a "structural differential" with which to represent visually the major G. S. principles. A partial reproduction of it is shown on the following page.

The circle at B represents an object, person, or event as we see it, or sense it. Each hole in the circle represents one characteristic of that object, person, or event.

Let us use a lemon as an example. The lemon has color, weight, dimensions. It has a rind. It has seeds. It contains vitamin C. Each of these items is represented by a hole in the circle.

But if we were to study this same lemon with a microscope we would discover many other characteristics, invisible to normal sight. This same lemon at the microscopic level is represented by the U-shaped figure at A in the diagram. Each hole again represents a characteristic of the submicroscopic lemon. Some characteristics we know about; these are represented by the strings which lead from A to B. Some characteristics we have not yet discovered. These are shown by the strings that dangle.

The jagged edge on the top represents the present margin of scientific knowledge, which can be pushed farther and farther back as man progresses. And the lines of the U-shaped figure (mathematically known as a parabola) go off indefinitely—indicating a complex, constantly changing process. The rectangle at C represents the label or name we give this object: *lemon;* but, as is apparent from the diagram, the label does not fully represent the visible object, and far less represents the sub-microscopic or the atomic structure beyond the visible object. Thus it is seen how words only imperfectly and incompletely describe reality,

A PORTION OF KORZYBSKI'S
STRUCTURAL DIFFERENTIAL

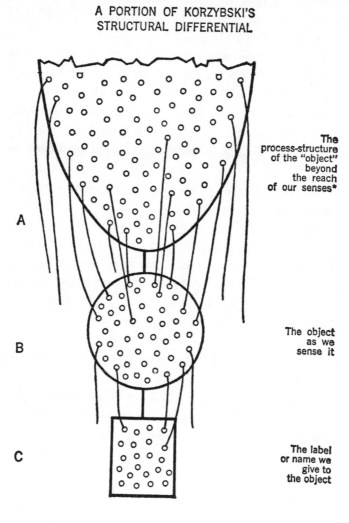

The
process-structure
of the "object"
beyond
the reach
of our senses*

A

The object
as we
sense it

B

The label
or name we
give to
the object

C

* as it is provisionally assumed to occur by science

and how knowledge acquired through the senses very imperfectly and incompletely reflects the truth. Any object is infinite, though we call it "finite." The imperceptible is a *reality* even though our senses pick up only a fragment of what is really there. By studying this diagram we can clearly see the truth of these statements. We are reminded of the folly of absolutism and of rigid opinions. We are shown the wisdom of open-mindedness and of humility.

Training with this diagram, and with the system as a whole, tends therefore to clarify thinking, reduce confusions, increase flexibility, diminish tensions. It is conducive to the scientific attitude. It opens the mind to the possibility of new knowledge and new points of view. I have seen these consequences occur again and again.

In only a few areas, notably parapsychology, religion, and reincarnation, have I found General Semanticists as a whole to be rather closed-minded. This is understandable, I suppose. They are merely sharing in the general intellectual blind spots of our hemisphere. For the most part it has never occurred to them to investigate these subjects.

But if they continue to be closed-minded and hostile to these subjects (and some of them are hostile), it will surprise me greatly. It will surprise me because such an attitude goes quite contrary both to the spirit and to the implications of their own methodology.

General Semantics, as defined by Korzybski himself, is an epistemological system—that is to say, it is concerned with the origins of knowledge. If knowledge is obtainable by ways other than the five senses—and there are vast quantities of evidence to show that it is—then General

Semanticists are not being very thorough or very up-to-date if they continue to neglect the work of parapsychologists who have studied the materials and methods of this unorthodox kind of knowledge. Moreover, by holding aloof from it, they are acting strangely contrary to their own basic principle of non-allness, which states that nobody (not even a General Semanticist) knows everything about anything. What is more, they are failing to recognize that their system provides a set of precision tools for thinking which can be applied to *any* field of human interest, and which can be of particular usefulness in the field of the psychic and the paranormal, which is often so slippery and so filled with treacherous pitfalls for the unwary.

The same considerations hold with regard to religion. Perhaps 95 per cent of all General Semanticists regard religion with considerable distate. The attitude is perhaps understandable, in view of the fact that religion almost always takes its origin from some Authority rather than from scientific demonstration; much of religion deals with matters not at present completely susceptible of scientific verification; and among the followers of almost all religions there exist many tragic confusions and misevaluations.

But here again the aloofness of the General Semanticists is regrettable. If they could only overcome their disdain long enough to take a careful look, they might find the great religions of the world fascinating if only because they contain so many historical illustrations of some very grave semantic confusions. Moreover, the trained General Semanticist could make an immeasurably important contribution to civilization if he used his tools of thought to analyze these confusions. Lacking mystical or transcendental experience himself, and lacking a knowledge of parapsychological phenomena, he might be incapable of understanding some of the basic propositions of religion and some of its manifestations; but within certain limits he could separate the wheat from the chaff, the authentic from the spurious, the sane from the insane; and as a result we might have more faith, more hope, and more clarity as well as more charity in the world.

In addition, General Semanticists could learn something of real importance to themselves and of real relevance to their own concerns if they would only devote a little study to the great religious systems of the world. Hinduism and Buddhism would be particularly fruitful areas of study, as both of them contain statements, made centuries ago, which are parallel to the statements of modern physicists and to those of Korzybski.

In the past few years articles have appeared from time to time in the General Semantics magazines, *Etc.* and the *General Semantics Bulletin,* that have shown certain similarities between Zen Buddhism and General Semantics; but up until recently most General Semanticists seem to have regarded these similarities as only of passing interest. This is unfortunate, because the parallels between General Semantics and the whole stream of Buddhist thought are, I am convinced, not of incidental but of primary importance.

Like most other people in our part of the world, General Semanticists do not know that 2600 years ago Buddha thought and spoke in a remarkably rational and scientific manner.

Here is an interesting paragraph:

Do not believe in what you have heard; do not believe in traditions because they have been handed down for many generations; do not believe in anything because it is rumored and spoken of by many; do not believe merely because the written statements of some old sage are produced; do not believe in conjectures; do not believe in that as truth to which you have become attached by habit; do not believe merely on the authority of your teachers and elders. After observation and analysis, when it agrees with reason and is conducive to the good and benefit of one and all, then accept it and live up to it.[6]

This sounds as if it came from a General Semantics textbook, or from the lecture of a twentieth-century scientist. It happens to be a statement made by Gautama Buddha. Again and again one can find passages in the Buddhist texts which are so strikingly parallel to the spirit of modern physics and General Semantics as to startle one.

I do not believe that this should be dismissed merely as a curious coincidence. I believe rather that it is indicative

[6] Quoted in *Three Lectures on the Vedanta Philosophy* by Max Muller (Longmans, Green, and Co., London, 1894).

of the fact that the science of the modern West and the philosophies of the ancient East are significantly related, even though separated by time and space. General Semantics can bridge this separation. General Semantics can make the philosophic riches of the East more comprehensible to the literal-minded West, and can help the poetic East to separate the wheat from the chaff in its own ancient traditions.

But here is another fact for General Semanticists to ponder. Buddha often stressed that all things are in a constant state of change; he spoke much about the deceptiveness of sense impressions and about the fallacies inherent in language; he frequently stated that the man who is not misled by false appearances, assumptions, and inferences obtains great strength. All of these points are routinely made in a General Semantics training course. But Buddha also referred frequently to reincarnation and karma. . . .

If a man tells us ten things, and nine of them we know to be true, should we then accept on faith the tenth thing? Not at all. But we should give the tenth thing some intelligent scrutiny at least.

The theory of reincarnation and the methodology of General Semantics, then, are my two proposals to the world.

They are vastly different approaches. Yet both are scientific in spirit. Both have compelling ethical consequences. Both lead to a synthesis of philosophic, scientific, psychological, and religious thought. Both constitute a bridge between the science of the West and the wisdom of the East.

Both are conducive to *unity*—unity of man within himself, and unity of man with other men.

Thus, both in their way can do much toward inducing a greater sanity on this mad, sad planet.

I recommend them earnestly, and urgently, to your attention.

SOME RECOMMENDED READING

CHAPTER 1

Bernstein, Morey. *The Search for Bridey Murphy.* Doubleday and Co., N.Y., 1956. (See especially the new edition, scheduled for 1963.)

Dunlap, Jane. *Exploring Inner Space.* Harcourt, Brace, and World, N.Y., 1961.

Stevenson, Ian, Dr. "The Evidence for Survival from Claimed Memories of Former Incarnations," article published April and July, 1960, in the *Journal of the American Society for Psychical Research.* Reprints available from The Theosophical Press, Wheaton, Ill., and the A.R.E. Press, Virginia Beach, Va.

CHAPTER 2

Edwin, Ronald. *Clock Without Hands.* The Falcon's Wing Press, 1956.

Hurkos, Peter. *Psychic, The Story of Peter Hurkos.* Bobbs-Merrill, N.Y., 1961.

Marion, Frederick. *In My Mind's Eye.* Wehman Bros., N.Y., 1950.

Millard, Joseph. *Edgar Cayce, Man of Miracles.* Spearman, London, 1961.

Puharich, Andrija, Dr. *The Sacred Mushroom.* Doubleday & Co., Garden City, N.Y., 1959.

Also: NBC's Monitor National Radio Show on the Edgar Cayce Story, a 33⅓ LP record of 15-minute interviews with people who knew Cayce's work personally.

CHAPTER 3

Ducasse, C. W. *A Critical Examination of the Belief in Life after Death.* C. C. Thomas, Springfield, Ill., 1960.
Kingsland, Wm. *The Real H. P. Blavatsky.*[1] John L. Watkins, London, 1928.
Kline, Milton V., Ed. *A Scientific Report on the Search for Bridey Murphy.* The Julian Press, N.Y., 1956.
Sinnett, A. P. *Incidents in the Life of Mme. Blavatsky.*[1] The Theosophical Publishing Society, London, 1913.

CHAPTER 4

Jinarajadasa, C. *How We Remember Our Past Lives.*[2] The Theosophical Publishing House, Adyar, Madras, India, 1955.
Low, Abraham, A., M.D. *Mental Health through Will Training.* The Christopher Publishing House, Boston, Mass., 1950.
Regardie, Israel. *The Romance of Metaphysics.* Ariel Press, Chicago, Ill., 1946.
Salter, Andrew. *Conditioned Reflex Therapy.* The Creative Age Press, N.Y., 1949.

CHAPTER 5

Sorokin, Pitirim. *The Ways and Power of Love.* The Beacon Press, Boston, Mass., 1954.

[1] Almost all Theosophical books are available from: The Theosophical Press, Wheaton, Ill. Catalogue on request.
[2] See footnote Chapter 3.

CHAPTER 6

Barrett, Wm. *Flight From Youth*. Doubleday & Co., N.Y., 1960.

Blavatsky, H. P. *Key To Theosophy*. Theosophical Publishing House, Adyar, Madras, India, 1933.

Gibran, Kahlil. *The Prophet*. Alfred A. Knopf, N.Y., 1955.

Haggard, Rider. *She*. Books, Inc., N.Y., 1887.

Head, Joseph, and Cranston, S. L. *Reincarnation, An East-West Anthology*. The Julian Press, N.Y., 1961.

London, Jack. *The Star Rover*. The Macmillan Co., N.Y., 1919.

Maugham, Somerset. *The Razor's Edge*. Doubleday, Doran, N.Y., 1943.

Salinger, J. D. "Teddy," in *Nine Stories*. Little, Brown and Co., Boston, Mass., 1948.

Scott, Cyril. *The Initiate*. Low, Brydone, London, 1920.

———. *The Initiate in the New World*. E. P. Dutton & Co., N.Y., 1927.

Whitman, Walt. *Leaves of Grass*. David McKay, Philadelphia, 1900.

CHAPTER 7

Adamson, Joy. *Born Free*. Pantheon Books, N.Y., 1960.

Boone, J. Allen. *Kinship with All Life*. Harper & Bros., N.Y., 1954.

———. *Letters to Strongheart*. Prentice-Hall, Inc., N.Y., 1939.

Colette (Mme. Jouvenal). *Creatures Great and Small*. Farrar, Straus & Cudahy, N.Y.

Dunstan, Patricia Raymond. *Manual on Vivisection*. Calore Publications, P.O. Box 17403, Foy Station, Los Angeles, Calif.

Dunlap, Jane. *Exploring Inner Space*. Harcourt, Brace, and World, N.Y., 1961.

Hume, Douglas, E. *The Mind Changers.* The Garden City Press, Ltd., Letchworth, Hertfordshire, England, 1939.

Joy, Charles, ed. *The Animal World of Albert Schweitzer.* The Beacon Press, Boston, Mass., 1950.

Lambert, Joyce. *How To Be Kind.* Brunswick Press Ltd., Fredericton, N.B., Canada, 1962. (Manual for The Kindness Club)

Nichols, Beverly. *Cats' ABC.* E. P. Dutton and Co., N.Y., 1960.

Packard, Vance. *Animal IQ.* Dial Press, N.Y., 1950.

Sarton, May. *The Fur Person.* Rinehart and Co., N.Y., 1957.

Steele, Zulma. *Angel in Top Hat.* Harper and Bros., N.Y., 1942.

Also: The magazine *Voice of the Voiceless,* published by Calore Publications, P.O. Box 17403 Foy Station, Los Angeles 17, Calif. $2 a year.

CHAPTER 8

Haney, William. *Communication: Patterns and Incidents.* Richard D. Irwin, Inc., Homewood, Ill., 1960.

Keyes, Kenneth. *How to Develop Your Thinking Ability.* McGraw-Hill Book Co., N.Y., 1950.

Korzybski, Alfred. *Science and Sanity: An Introduction to Non-Aristotelian Systems and General Semantics.* International Non-Aristotelian Library Publishing Co. (1st ed. 1933, 4th ed. 1958); distributed by Institute of General Semantics, Lakeville, Conn.

Lee, Irving. *Language Habits in Human Affairs.* Harper & Bros., N.Y., 1941.

Lee, Irving, and Lee, Laura. *Handling Barriers in Communication.* Harper & Bros., N.Y., 1956.

Minteer, Catherine. *Words and What They Do to You.* Row, Peterson, and Co., Evanston, Ill., 1953.

Also: *Etc.: A Review of General Semantics,* published 4 times
 a year. Editorial office: San Francisco State College, San
 Francisco 27, Calif.
The General Semantics Bulletin, published for members of
 the Institute. Institute of General Semantics, Lakeville,
 Conn.

INDEX